THREE PLAYS

BY

D. H. LAWRENCE

David Herbert Lawrence was born at Eastwood, Nottingham-
shire, in 1885, fourth of the five children of a miner and his
middle-class wife. He attended Nottingham High School and
Nottingham University College. His first novel, *The White
Peacock*, was published in 1911, just a few weeks after the death
of his mother to whom he had been abnormally close. At this
time he finally ended his relationship with Jessie Chambers
(the Miriam of *Sons and Lovers*) and became engaged to Louie
Burrows. His career as a schoolteacher was ended in 1911 by
the illness which was ultimately diagnosed as tuberculosis.

In 1912 Lawrence eloped to Germany with Frieda Weekley,
the German wife of his former modern languages tutor. They
were married on their return to England in 1914. Lawrence was
now living, precariously, by his writing. His greatest novels,
The Rainbow and *Women in Love*, were completed in 1915 and
1916. The former was suppressed, and he could not find a pub-
lisher for the latter.

After the war Lawrence began his 'savage pilgrimage' in
search of a more fulfilling mode of life than industrial Western
civilization could offer. This took him to Sicily, Ceylon,
Australia and, finally, New Mexico. The Lawrences returned to
Europe in 1925. Lawrence's last novel, *Lady Chatterley's Lover*,
was banned in 1928, and his paintings confiscated in 1929. He
died in Vence in 1930 at the age of fourty-four.

Lawrence spent most of his short life living. Nevertheless he
produced an amazing quantity of work – novels, stories, poems,
plays, essays, travel books, translations, and letters ... After
his death Frieda wrote: 'What he had seen and felt and known
he gave in his writing to his fellow men, the splendour of
living, the hope of more and more life ... a heroic and im-
measurable gift.'

THREE PLAYS

BY

D. H. LAWRENCE

A COLLIER'S FRIDAY NIGHT

THE DAUGHTER-IN-LAW

THE WIDOWING OF
MRS HOLROYD

WITH AN INTRODUCTION
BY RAYMOND WILLIAMS

PENGUIN BOOKS

Penguin Books Ltd, Harmondsworth, Middlesex, England
Penguin Books Inc., 7110 Ambassador Road, Baltimore, Maryland 21207, U.S.A.
Penguin Books Australia Ltd, Ringwood, Victoria, Australia
Penguin Books Canada Ltd, 41 Steelcase Road West, Markham, Ontario, Canada

—

This collection first published in Penguin Books 1969
Reprinted 1971, 1974

—

From *The Complete Plays of D. H. Lawrence*, copyright © the Estate of the late Mrs
Frieda Lawrence, 1965. All rights reserved. Reprinted by arrangement with William
Heinemann Ltd and The Viking Press, Inc.
This collection copyright © the Estate of the late Mrs Frieda Lawrence, 1969
Introduction copyright © Raymond Williams, 1969
All inquiries regarding performance rights of these plays should be
directed to Margery Vosper Ltd, 54A Shaftesbury Avenue, London, W1

—

Made and printed in Great Britain
by Hazell Watson & Viney Ltd
Aylesbury, Bucks
Set in Monotype Garamond

CONTENTS

INTRODUCTION

by Raymond Williams

LAWRENCE was a teacher in Croydon, twenty-four years old, when he wrote his first play, *A Collier's Friday Night*. That year (1909) was important in his attempt to establish himself as a writer; he got his first professional publication, with a group of poems in the November issue of the *English Review*. He had been writing for five years, while qualifying as a teacher. He had left Nottingham High School at sixteen, and gone to work for three months as a clerk in a factory. After a serious illness, he had begun pupil-teaching in the mining village, Eastwood, where he was born, and when he was eighteen (in 1903) went to the Pupil-Teacher Centre at Ilkeston for a year, and came out first in the country in the King's Scholarship examination. In that same year he wrote his first poems. He went back to Eastwood for a year's uncertificated teaching, saving money for his fees at University College, Nottingham, which he entered for a two-year course in 1906. During that year at Eastwood he began his first novel, eventually published as *The White Peacock*. When he had got his teacher's certificate, in 1908, he took the job at a new elementary school in Croydon for a hundred pounds a year. He stayed in this job until he again became ill at the end of 1911. His mother had died at the end of 1910, but had seen an advance copy of his first book, *The White Peacock*, published in January 1911. In the rest of that year, Lawrence wrote the first draft of his second novel (*The Trespasser*, then called *The Saga of Siegmund*), more poems and stories, and two more plays, *The Daughter-in-Law* and *The Widowing of Mrs Holroyd*. After he was forced to give up teaching, he rewrote *The Trespasser*, which was published in May 1912, and began the first draft of his third novel (*Sons and Lovers*, then called *Paul Morel*), which was eventually published in 1913. Meanwhile, in April 1912, he had met Frieda Weekley, and in May went with her to Germany and then Italy, until April 1913. During that year abroad, he wrote the final version of *Sons and Lovers*, more poems and stories and essays, began the novel *The Sisters* which was eventually to become *The Rainbow* and *Women in Love*, and wrote three more plays, *The Fight for Barbara*, *The Merry-go-Round* and *The Married Man*. He was not to write plays again until much later in his life. None of them had been produced, and only one, *The Widowing of Mrs Holroyd*, had been published (in 1914). He wanted to revise this play when it was at last produced in London in 1926, but did not. He was by then known mainly as a novelist, though he still wrote in many forms – poems, essays and sketches – and in 1920 wrote another play – *Touch and Go*, following a character from *Women in Love* – and in 1925 his last play, *David*.

It is important to remember this order of events, as we read these plays. When a writer has become famous, and his main achievements are known, it is very easy to read his growth backwards, from the success to the development. But when Lawrence began writing plays during his period of teaching at Croydon he could not really know in which ways his gifts, and even more his opportunities, would develop. We tend to read the plays now when we already know the novelist, and some people have argued that he was 'always a novelist', even 'a born novelist', and that what they call his 'attempts' at plays were a sideline, or even a mistake he got over. But we then have to say that for a writer like Lawrence nothing was a sideline. From the time he began writing, he was always experimenting, always ready to try his hand. Of the plays he finished, *The Married Man* and *The Merry-go-Round* are, as he described them in a letter (14 November 1912), 'impromptus'. But he had put his heart into the others, and wanted them to succeed. To see why they had to wait more than half a century for any general recognition we have to look not only at the plays but at the opportunities, in the general condition of English drama and theatre.

The plays of the first period – *A Collier's Friday Night*, *The Daughter-in-Law* and *The Widowing of Mrs Holroyd* – were written in the three years at Croydon after he had moved away from the mining village where he was born and had grown up. He went back to Eastwood during that time for holidays and at occasional weekends. During his mother's long illness, which had so great an effect on him, he was back more often. In the novels of this period – *The White Peacock* and *The Trespasser* – Lawrence was in important ways unable to deal with his central experiences, or with the life that was nearest to him. His final resolution of this early crisis was indeed in the great novel *Sons and Lovers*, but his first direct attempts to write this experience were in plays and stories: often a play and a story on the same experience, as with *The Widowing of Mrs Holroyd* and *The Odour of Chrysanthemums*. *A Collier's Friday Night*, very clearly, is a first writing of some of the central experience of *Sons and Lovers*. *The Daughter-in-Law* is a sustained look at the interaction of family relationships and the mining crisis, outside his personal situation. He was not, that is to say, writing the plays as a sideline, or as theatrical versions of his fiction. He was trying many forms, all comparatively short, in which this decisive experience – of love, of a family, of working life – could be shaped and written.

We have few precise details of the dates of writing, or of such relations as there were between plays, stories and drafts of novels. We know that Lawrence showed Jessie Chambers (the 'Miriam' of *Sons and Lovers*) a copy of *A Collier's Friday Night* when she visited him in Croydon in the autumn of 1909. This was in any case a critical meeting between them. Some time between then and the autumn of 1911 he wrote the other two plays. In a letter to Edward Garnett (6 October 1911) Lawrence wrote:

I send you this, the one play I have at home. I have written to Mr Hueffer (editor of the *English Review*) for the other two. This is the least literary – and the least unified of the three. I tried to write for the stage – I tried to make it end up stagily . . . The first scenes are good.

We do not know which play this was – probably *The Widowing of Mrs Holroyd* – but clearly all three had been written by this time. Discussing plays in a letter of the same month, Lawrence referred to his own 'ravels of detail' and wanted a 'clean bareness', but was still hoping that the plays would be published in a volume in the spring. In November he wrote to Garnett:

Hueffer seems actually to have lost the other two plays. It's a nuisance.

We hear no more of the plays until 1913.

Lawrence had been going to the theatre in London while at Croydon, but like so many young writers found publication much easier than any theatrical contact. He sent the plays, almost naturally, to be published rather than produced: that was the most available opportunity. But he had been reading other dramatists: Synge from as early as 1909, and in April 1911 – perhaps at about the time when the second and third plays were being written – he wrote to Mrs Hopkin:

Riders to the Sea is about the genuinest bit of dramatic tragedy, English, since Shakespeare, I should say.

When he returned to the possibility of drama, with his second group of three plays written in 1912, he wrote in a letter to Garnett (1 February 1913):

I believe that, just as an audience was found in Russia for Tchekhov, so an audience might be found in England for some of my stuff, if there were a man to whip 'em in. It's the producer that is lacking, not the audience. I am sure we are sick of the rather bony, bloodless drama we get nowadays – it is time for a reaction against Shaw and Galsworthy and Barker and Irishy (except Synge) people – the rule and measure mathematical folk. But you are of them, and your sympathies are with your own generation, not with mine. I think it is inevitable. You are about the only man who is willing to let a new generation come in. It will seem a bit rough to me, when I am 45, and must see myself and my tradition supplanted. I shall bear it very badly. Damn my impudence, but don't dislike me. But I don't want to write like Galsworthy nor Ibsen, nor Strindberg, nor any of them, not even if I could. We have to hate our immediate predecessors, to get free from their authority.

There is a strange and characteristic unease in the turns of this

letter, but in his main points Lawrence is very clear. In rejecting Shaw and Galsworthy and Granville Barker he was
rejecting the only body of serious new drama in England, in
his immediate period, from the Vedrenne–Barker productions
at the Royal Court theatre between 1904 and 1907. That, in
England, was the new drama, and was mobilizing minority
support; in European terms, it was attaching itself to a version
of Ibsen. Lawrence's rejection of it was inevitable: what he
meant by 'rule and measure mathematical folk' was the drama
of abstract ideas and representative problems, and he was
against this not only because it was 'bony, bloodless' but also
because it so clearly belonged to a different social world from
his own. Its basis, as in all the European free theatres of the
time, was a middle-class critique of a middle-class view of the
world; the experiences, and the problems, of the working
people among whom Lawrence grew up were either absent
or caricatured, as most notably in a Fabian socialist like Shaw.
Lawrence is equally clear in his identification of relevant
predecessors: Synge, obviously, because there was drama
based on the experience and the talk of ordinary people;
Chekhov, because there was a relevant dramatic form –
dismissed by some theorists of the new drama as formless –
in which the interaction of personal relationships and social
pressures was expressed in a seamless, apparently haphazard,
pattern of voices. These points give us the necessary clues to
Lawrence's first three plays, which are based on one of the
variant forms of high naturalism: the play which gets close to
ordinary experience, not only by taking ordinary situations
and probable characters, but by using these to embody crises
of immediate relationships, with an emphasis on ways of
speaking, minutely observed and reproduced, as the social
reality of a particular dimension of life. This is critically
different from the use of ordinary situations, probable
characters and probable conversation to embody a problem
capable of being stated in general terms, or, in the action
itself, of being debated: the method, most obviously, of
Galsworthy, and of what was known and, under Shaw's
influence, understood, of Ibsen. It is different, also, from the

naturalism of Strindberg, with whom Lawrence has so much otherwise in common; for what Strindberg had done was to isolate the crises of immediate relationship from the context of ordinary or supporting reality: steadily cutting away subsidiary characters, situations, experiences, so that the crisis could be played directly; and finally, in his later plays, inventing a form beyond naturalism in which the crisis created not only the place and the situation, but the characters and the quality of the speech, which were no longer probable in terms of observed reality, but only in their expression of a crisis which spanned visible and hidden experience.

Lawrence's option, then, was for one particular kind of naturalism. To call the plays naturalist, without this further definition, is useless. There is an intense attachment to the importance of ordinary experience, and this is seen, in a single dimension, as both social and personal. But the dramatic reality is created by a scrupulous fidelity to the way people talk, in this place and this situation: not probable dialogue, in stage terms, but the dramatic action coming out of these rhythms which are the shapes of particular lives and of a common life. Chekhov, in a very different place and situation, had made the same choice; so, even to listening through the floorboards, had Synge. But the compatibility of this action with the expectations of the theatre was never easy. Chekhov had steadily to cut out what he called the pistol-shot: the theatrical resolution, but also the cutting-off, of a flow of life. And as Lawrence said later, on the same point:

To me even Synge, whom I admire very much indeed, is a bit too rounded off, and, as it were, put on the shelf to be looked at. I can't bear art you can walk round and admire.

In a theatre, both popular and minority, in which the presentation and rounding-off of experience were habitual, such an emphasis on flow, incompleteness, unfinished rhythms because the lives were unfinished, would not easily be accepted as 'dramatic' at all. Trying to adapt to the stage, Lawrence put into *The Widowing of Mrs Holroyd* what would 'end up stagily' – the scene of the washing of the dead body – and apologized that the other plays were 'literary', with too many 'ravels of detail'. Revising the play in 1913, he wrote:

I saw how it needed altering, refining. Particularly I hated it in the last act, where the man and woman wrangled rather shallowly across the dead body of the husband. And it seemed nasty that they should make love where he lay drunk. I hope to heaven I have come in time to have it made decent.

The terms of the judgement are significant. It is the feeling that matters, but Lawrence was stuck with a theatrical pressure to unify, within a fixed place, a fixed room, on the stage, and with the conventional need for a single overall crisis. Within those pressures, his solution was brilliant, but the problem of form remained.

Instead of saying now, conventionally, that Lawrence was always 'really a novelist', and that the plays are of that kind, we ought to say that here a writer of genius, at a very early stage of his work, met and identified a major problem of modern dramatic form: the contradiction between the detail and closeness of fiction, through which the flow of experience and the sympathy with ordinary life and speech could be practically achieved, and the habits of theatre, and of most traditional drama, in which posture, rhetoric, formality and presentation, over the whole immense range from the greatest drama to the most conventional boulevard piece, had been the ordinary means. That this problem is still unsolved is evident from the movement of so much of our best drama away from ordinary experience and away from the flow of sympathy; the counter-movement, in part in the theatre, but mainly in film and in television, has only just begun. Lawrence could not solve the problem on his own; there was no theatre in England which could remotely understand what he was trying to do. In his later plays, he moved to a brittle stagey talk, as in the three of 1912, or to stage discussion of a presented kind, as in *Touch and Go*, or, finally, in the direction of so many writers, to the traditional, reminiscent, scriptural rhythms of *David*. But there had been a moment, when these three first plays were being written, when a new English dramatist was ready to engage with his audience, in a theatre of ordinary feeling raised to intensity and community by the writing of ordinary speech, and when it was the institutions – the links between writer and audience – which were absent, during the occupation of the theatre by a different class and form. It is very significant that now, half a century later, Lawrence's stories of that period can be brilliantly dramatized for television (as in the Granada series), and that, in another Royal Court season, the links and so the audience can at last be found.

Given that frustration, of course, at so early and difficult a time, Lawrence didn't get past his first experiments. He brought to the drama a capacity for the rhythms of speech – as most notably in *The Daughter-in-Law* – which in the end he developed to change not only the dialogue but the narrative and analytic tones of the English novel. Stuck in a room, as the only modern drama he knew then was, he had to check the flow of action and of feeling at door and window, with that shaping social landscape of mine and railway and farm left outside, for description or report: a dramatic limitation that with the mobility of the film or television camera he could now surpass. I have discussed the detailed effects of this on the success of his plays, and on their relations with his fiction, in an essay in *Drama from Ibsen to Brecht*. But here, acknowledging the limitations – at once general and particular: the form, and the period and circumstances of the writing – the point to emphasize is that these plays show us that we have lost half a century. For what Lawrence was then trying to do, and what hardly anyone knew he had done, is what for the last ten or fifteen years a generation of writers has been again attempting, in a changing but still frustrating society. So that now we read *A Collier's Friday Night*, *The Daughter-in-Law*, *The Widowing of Mrs Holroyd*, of course as the early plays of a great novelist, but also as the work of a man who feels like a contemporary: a man who got ill, whose scripts were lost, who went on to do what there was a better chance of doing and did it magnificently; but whose early voice – the voice of that mining country – has survived against the odds, and can be so strongly heard.

In several cases alternative drafts of the plays in this volume exist in manuscript form, but the versions here printed are regarded as being the most complete.

The date in brackets under the title of each play indicates the year of completion of the text.

A COLLIER'S FRIDAY NIGHT

A PLAY IN THREE ACTS
(About 1909 – first published 1934)

CHARACTERS

MRS LAMBERT
LAMBERT
NELLIE LAMBERT
ERNEST LAMBERT
MAGGIE PEARSON
GERTIE COOMBER
BEATRICE WYLD
BARKER
CARLIN

The action of the play takes place in the kitchen of the Lamberts' house.

ACT ONE

The kitchen or living-room of a working-man's house. At the back the fireplace, with a large fire burning. On the left, on the oven side of the stove, a woman of some fifty-five years sits in a wooden rocking-chair, reading. Behind her and above her, in the recess made by the fireplace, four shelves of books, the shelf-covers being of green serge, with woollen ball fringe, and the books being ill-assorted school books, with an edition of Lessing, florid in green and gilt, but tarnished. On the left, a window looking on a garden where the rain is dripping through the first twilight. Under the window, a sofa, the bed covered with red chintz. By the side of the window, on the wall near the ceiling, a quiver clothes-horse is outspread with the cotton articles which have been ironed, hanging to air. Under the outspread clothes is the door which communicates with the scullery and with the yard. On the right side of the fireplace, in the recess equivalent to that where the bookshelves stand, a long narrow window, and below it, a low, brown, fixed cup-board, whose top forms a little sideboard, on which stand a large black enamel box of oil-colours, and a similar japanned box of water-colours, with Reeve's silver trade-mark. There is also on the cupboard top a tall glass jar containing ragged pink chrysanthemums. On the right is a bookcase upon a chest of drawers. This piece of furniture is of stained polished wood in imitation of mahogany. The upper case is full of books, seen through the two flimsy glass doors: a large set of the World's Famous Literature in dark green at the top – then on the next shelf prize-books in calf and gold, and imitation soft leather poetry-books, and a Nuttall's dictionary and Cassell's French, German and Latin dictionaries. On each side of the bookcase are prints from water-colours, large, pleasing and well framed in oak. Between the little brown cupboard and the bookcase, an arm-chair, small, round, with many little staves; a comfortable chair such as is seen in many working-class kitchens; it has a red chintz cushion. There is another Windsor chair on the other side of the bookcase. Over the mantelpiece, which is high, with brass candlesticks and two 'Coronation' tumblers in enamel, hangs a picture of Venice, from one of Stead's Christmas Numbers – nevertheless, satisfactory enough.

The woman in the rocking-chair is dressed in black, and wears a black sateen apron. She wears spectacles, and is reading The New Age. *Now and again she looks over her paper at a piece of bread which stands on a hanging bar before the fire, propped up by a fork, toasting. There is a little pile of toast on a plate on the boiler hob beside a large saucepan; the kettle and a brown teapot are occupying the oven-top near the woman. The table is laid for tea, with four large breakfastcups in dark-blue willow-pattern, and plates similar. It is an oval mahogany table, large enough to seat eight comfortably. The woman sees the piece of bread smoking, and takes it from the fire. She butters it and places it on the plate on the hob, after which she looks out of the window, then, taking her paper, sits down again in her place.*

Someone passes the long narrow window, only the head being seen, then quite close to the large window on the left. There is a noise as the outer door opens and is shut, then the kitchen door opens, and a girl enters. She is tall and thin, and wears a long grey coat and a large blue hat, quite plain. After glancing at the table, she crosses the room, drops her two exercise-books on the wooden chair by the bookcase, saying:

NELLIE LAMBERT: Oh! I am weary.

MOTHER: You are late.

NELLIE: I know I am. It's Agatha Karton – she is a great gaby. There's always something wrong with her register, and old Tommy gets in such a fever, the great kid. [*She takes off her hat, and going to the door on right, stands in the doorway, hanging it up with her coat on the pegs in the passage, just by the doorway.*] And I'm sure the youngsters have been regular little demons; I could have killed them.

MOTHER: I've no doubt they felt the same towards you, poor little wretches.

NELLIE [*with a short laugh*]: I'll bet they did, for I spanked one or two of 'em well.

MOTHER: Trust you, trust you! You'll be getting the mothers if you're not careful.

NELLIE [*contemptuously*]: I had one old cat this afternoon. But I told her straight. I said: 'If your Johnny, or Sammy, or whatever he is, is a nuisance, he'll be smacked, and there's an end of it.' She was mad, but I told her straight; I didn't care. She can go to Tommy if she likes: I know he'll fuss her round, but I'll tell *him* too. Pah! he fusses the creatures up! – I *would*! [*She comes towards the table, pushing up her hair with her fingers. It is heavy and brown, and has been flattened by her hat. She glances at herself in the little square mirror which hangs from a nail under the right end of the mantelpiece, a mere unconscious glance which betrays no feeling, and is just enough to make her negligently touch her hair again. She turns a trifle fretfully to the table.*]

NELLIE: Is there only potted meat? You know I can't bear it.

MOTHER [*conciliatorily*]: Why, I thought you'd like it, a raw day like this – and with toast.

NELLIE: You know I don't. Why didn't you get some fruit? – a little tin of apricots –

MOTHER: I thought you'd be sick of apricots – I know Ernest is.

NELLIE: Well, I'm not – you know I'm not. Pappy potted meat! [*She sits down on the sofa wearily. Her* MOTHER *pours out two cups of tea, and replaces the pot on the hob.*]

MOTHER: Won't you have some, then?

NELLIE [*petulantly*]: No, I don't want it.

[*The* MOTHER *stands irresolute a moment, then she goes out.* NELLIE *reaches over to the bookshelves and takes a copy of* The Scarlet Pimpernel, *which she opens on the table, and reads, sipping her tea but not eating. In a moment or two she glances up, as the* MOTHER *passes the window and enters the scullery. There is the sound of the opening of a tin.*]

NELLIE: Have you fetched some? – Oh, you are a sweetling! [*The* MOTHER *enters, with a little glass dish of small tinned apricots. They begin tea.*]

MOTHER: Polly Goddard says her young man got hurt in the pit this morning.

NELLIE: Oh – is it much? [*She looks up from her book.*]

MOTHER: One of his feet crushed. Poor Polly's very sad. What made her tell me was Ben Goddard going by. I didn't know he was at work again, but he was just coming home, and I asked her about him, and then she went on to tell me of her young man. They're all coming home from Selson, so I expect your father won't be long.

NELLIE: Goodness! – I hope he'll let us get our tea first.

MOTHER: Well, you were late. If he once gets seated in the Miner's Arms there's no telling when he comes.

NELLIE: I don't care when he does, so long as he doesn't come yet.

MOTHER: Oh, it's all very well!

[*They both begin to read as they eat. After a moment another girl runs past the window and enters. She is a plump, fair girl, pink and white. She has just run across from the next house.*]

GERTIE COOMBER: Hello, my duck, and how are you?

NELLIE [*looking up*]: Oh, alright, my bird.

GERTIE: Friday to-night. No Eddie for you! Oh, poor Nellie! Aren't *I* glad, though! [*She snaps her fingers quaintly.*]

[*The* MOTHER *laughs.*]

NELLIE: Mean cat!

GERTIE [*giggling*]: No, I'm not a mean cat. But I like Friday night; we can go jinking off up town and wink at the boys. I like market night. [*She puts her head on one side in a peculiar, quaint, simple fashion.*]

[*The* MOTHER *laughs.*]

NELLIE: *You* wink! If she so much as sees a fellow who'd speak to her, she gets behind me and stands on one foot and then another.

GERTIE: I don't! No, I don't, Nellie Lambert. I go like this: 'Oh, good evening, *how* are you? I'm sure I'm very pleased –' [*She says this in a very quaint 'prunes-and-prisms' manner, with her chin in the air and her hand extended. At the end she giggles.*]

[*The* MOTHER, *with her cup in her hand, leans back and laughs.* NELLIE, *amused in spite of herself, smiles shortly.*]

NELLIE: You are a daft object! What about last week, when David Thompson –

[GERTIE *puts her hand up and flips the air with affected contempt.*]

GERTIE: David Thompson! A bacon sawyer! Ph!

NELLIE: What a name! Not likely. Mrs Grocock! [*She giggles.*] Oh dear no, nothing short of Mrs Carooso. [*She holds back the skirts of her long pinafore with one hand and affects the Gibson bend.*]

MOTHER [*laughing heartily*]: Caruso! Caruso! A great fat fellow – !

GERTIE: Besides, a collier! I'm not going to wash stinking pit-things.

NELLIE: You don't know what you'll do yet, my girl. I never knew such cheek! I should think you want somebody grand, you do.

GERTIE: I do that. Somebody who'll say, 'Yes, dear. Oh *yes*, dear! Certainly, certainly!' [*She simpers across the room, then giggles.*]

NELLIE: You soft cat, you! But look here, Gert, you'll get paid out, treating Bernard Hufton as you do.

GERTIE [*suddenly irritated*]: Oh, I can't abide him. I always feel as if I could smack his face. He thinks himself slikey. He always makes my –

[*A head passes the narrow side window.*]

Oh, glory! there's Mr Lambert. I'm off! [*She draws back against the bookcase. A man passes the large window. The door opens and he enters. He is a man of middling stature, a miner, black from the pit. His shoulders are pushed up because he is cold. He has a bushy iron-grey beard. He takes from his pocket a tin bottle and a knotted 'snap' bag – his food bag of dirty calico – and puts them with a bang on the table. Then he drags his heavily-shod feet to the door on right; he limps slightly, one leg being shorter than the other. He hangs up his coat and cap in the passage and comes back into the living-room. No one speaks. He wears a grey-and-black neckerchief and, being coatless, his black arms are bare to the elbows, where end the loose dirty sleeves of his flannel singlet. The MOTHER rises and goes to the scullery, carrying the heavy saucepan. The man gets hold of the table and pulls it nearer the fire, away from his daughter.*]

NELLIE: Why can't you leave the table where it was! We don't *want* it stuck on top of the fire.

FATHER: Ah dun, if you dunna. [*He drags up his arm-chair and sits down at the table full in front of the fire.*] 'An yer got a drink for me?

[*The* MOTHER *comes and pours out a cup of tea, then goes back to the scullery.*]

It's a nice thing as a man as comes home from th' pit parched up canna ha'e a drink got 'im. [*He speaks disagreeably.*]

MOTHER: Oh, you needn't begin! I know you've been stopping, drinking.

FATHER: Dun yer? – Well, yer know too much, then. You wiser than them as knows, you are!

[*There is a general silence, as if the three listeners were shrugging their shoulders in contempt and anger. The* FATHER *pours out his tea into his saucer, blows it and sucks it up.* NELLIE *looks up from her book and glowers at him with ferocity.* GERTIE *puts her hand before her mouth and giggles behind his back at the noise. He does not drink much, but sets the cup back in the saucer and lays his grimed arms wearily along the table. The* MOTHER *enters with a plate of cabbage.*]

MOTHER: Here, that's a clean cloth. [*She does not speak unkindly.*]

FATHER [*brutally*]: You should put a dotty (dirty) 'un on, then.

[*The* MOTHER *takes a newspaper and spreads it over the cloth before him. She kneels at the oven, takes out a stew-jar, and puts meat and gravy on the plate with the cabbage, and sets it before him. He does not begin at once to eat. The* MOTHER *puts back her chair against the wall and sits down.*]

MOTHER: Are your trousers wet?

FATHER [*as he eats*]: A bit.

MOTHER: Then why don't you take them off?

FATHER [*in a tone of brutal authority*]: Fetch my breeches an' wa's'coat down, Nellie.

NELLIE [*continuing to read, her hands pushed in among her hair*]: You can ask me properly.

[*The* FATHER *pushes his beard forward and glares at her with futile ferocity. She reads on.* GERTIE COOMBER, *at the back, shifts from one foot to the other, then coughs behind her hand as if she had a little cold. The* MOTHER *rises and goes out by door on right.*]

FATHER: You lazy, idle bitch, you let your mother go!

NELLIE [*shrugging her shoulders*]: You can shut up. [*She speaks with cold contempt.*]

[GERTIE *sighs audibly. The tension of the scene will not let her run home.* NELLIE *looks up, flushed, carefully avoiding her father.*]

NELLIE: Aren't you going to sit down, Gert?

GERTIE: No, I'm off.

NELLIE: Wait a bit and I'll come across with you. I don't want to stop *here*.

[*The* FATHER *stirs in his chair with rage at the implication. The* MOTHER *comes downstairs and enters with a pair of black trousers, from which the braces are trailing, and a black waistcoat lined with cream and red lining. She drops them against her husband's chair.*]

MOTHER [*kindly, trying to restore the atmosphere*]: Aren't you going to sit down, Gertie? Go on the stool.

[GERTIE *takes a small stool on the right side of fireplace, and sits toying with the bright brass tap of the boiler. The* MOTHER *goes out again on right, and enters immediately with five bread tins and a piece of lard paper. She stands on the hearth-rug greasing the tins. The* FATHER *kicks off his great boots and stands warming his trousers before the fire, turning them and warming them thoroughly.*]

GERTIE: Are they cold, Mr Lambert?

FATHER: They are that! Look you, they steaming like a sweating hoss.

MOTHER: Get away, man! The driest thing in the house would smoke if you held it in front of the fire like that.

FATHER [*shortly*]: Ah, I know I'm a liar. I knowed it to begin wi'.

NELLIE [*much irritated*]: Isn't he a nasty-tempered kid!

GERTIE: But those front bedrooms are clammy.

FATHER [*gratified*]: They h'are, Gertie, they h'are.

GERTIE [*turning to avoid* NELLIE'S *contempt and pottering the fire*]: I know the things I bring down from ours, they fair damp in a day.

FATHER: They h'are, Gertie, I know it. And I wonder how 'er'd like to clap 'er arse into wet breeches. [*He goes scrambling off to door on right, trailing his breeches.*]

NELLIE [*fiercely*]: Father!

[GERTIE *puts her face into her hands and laughs with a half-audible laugh that shakes her body.*]

I can't think what you've got to laugh at, Gertie Coomber. [*The* MOTHER, *glancing at her irate daughter, laughs also. She moves aside the small wooden rocking-chair, and, drawing forth a great panchion of dough from the corner under the bookshelves, begins to fill the bread tins. She sets them on the hearth – which has no fender, the day being Friday, when the steel fender is put away, after having been carefully cleaned, to be saved for Saturday afternoon. The* FATHER *enters, the braces of his trousers dangling, and drops the heavy moleskin pit breeches in corner on right.*]

NELLIE: I wonder why you can't put them in the scullery; the smell of them's hateful.

FATHER: You mun put up wi' it, then. If you were i' th' pit you'd niver put your nose up at them again. [*He sits down and recommences eating. The sound further irritates his daughter, who again pushes her fingers into her hair, covering her ears with her palms. Her father notices, and his manners become coarser.* NELLIE *rises, leaving her book open on the table.*]

NELLIE: Come on, Gert! [*She speaks with contemptuous impatience.*]

[*The* FATHER *watches them go out. He lays his arms along the newspaper, wearily.*]

FATHER: I'm too tired ter h'eat.

MOTHER [*sniffing, and hardening a little*]: I wonder why you always have to go and set her off in a tantrum as soon as you come in.

FATHER: A cheeky bitch; 'er wants a good slap at th' side o' th' mouth!

MOTHER [*incensed*]: If you've no more sense than that, I don't wonder –

FATHER: You don't wonder – you don't wonder! No, I know you don't wonder. It's you as eggs 'em on against me, both on 'em.

MOTHER [*scornfully*]: You set them against yourself. You do your best for it, every time they come in.

FATHER: Do I, do I! I set 'em against me, do I? I'm going to stand 'em orderin' me about, an' turnin' their noses up, am I?

MOTHER: You shouldn't make them turn their noses up, then. If you do your best for it, what do you expect?

FATHER: A jumped-up monkey! An' it's you as 'as made 'em like it, the pair on 'em. There's neither of 'em but what treats me like a dog. I'm not daft! I'm not blind! I can see it.

MOTHER: If you're so clever at seeing it, I should have thought you'd have sense enough not to begin it and carry it on as you do.

FATHER: Me begin it! When do I begin it? You niver hear me say a word to 'em, till they've snapped at me as if I was a – as if I was a – No, it's you as puts 'em on in. It's you, you blasted – [*He bangs the table with his fist. The* MOTHER *puts the bread in the oven, from which she takes a rice pudding; then she sits down to read. He glares across the table, then goes on eating. After a little while he pushes the plate from him. The* MOTHER *affects not to notice for a moment.*] 'An yer got any puddin'?

MOTHER: Have you finished? [*She rises, takes a plate and, crouching on the hearth, gives him his pudding. She glances at the clock, and clears the tea-things from her daughter's place. She puts another piece of toast down, there remaining only two pieces on the plate.*]

FATHER [*looking at the rice pudding*]: Is this what you'n had?

MOTHER: No; we had nothing.

FATHER: No, I'll bet you non 'ad this baby pap.

MOTHER: No, I had nothing for a change, and Nellie took her dinner.

FATHER [*eating unwillingly*]: Is there no other puddin' as you could 'a made?

MOTHER: Goodness, man, are you so mightily particular about your belly? This is the first rice pudding you've had for goodness knows how long, and – No, I couldn't make any other. In the first place, it's Friday, and in the second, I'd nothing to make it with.

FATHER: You wouldna ha'e, not for me. But if you 'a wanted –

MOTHER [*interrupting*]: You needn't say any more. The fact of the matter is, somebody's put you out at the pit, and you come home to vent your spleen on us.

FATHER [*shouting*]: You're a liar, you're a liar! A man comes home after a hard day's work to folks as 'as never a word to say to 'im, 'as shuts up the minute 'e enters the house, as 'ates the sight of 'im as soon as 'e comes in th' room – !

MOTHER [*with fierceness*]: We've had quite enough, we've had quite enough! Our Ernest'll be in in a minute and we're not going to have this row going on; he's coming home all the way from Derby, trailing from college to a house like this, tired out with study and all this journey: we're not going to have it, I tell you.

[*Her husband stares at her dumbly, betwixt anger and shame and sorrow, of which an undignified rage is predominant. The* MOTHER *carries out some pots to the scullery, re-enters, takes the slice of toast and butters it.*]

FATHER: It's about time as we had a light on it; I canna see what I'm eatin'.

[*The* MOTHER *puts down the toast on the hob, and having fetched a dustpan from the scullery, goes out on right to the cellar to turn on the gas and to bring coals. She is heard coming up the steps heavily. She mends the fire, and then lights the gas at a brass pendant hanging over the table. Directly after there enters a young man of twenty-one, tall and broad, pale, clean-shaven, with the brownish hair of the 'ginger' class, which is all ruffled when he has taken off his cap, after having pulled various books from his pockets and put them on the little cupboard top. He takes off his coat at door right as his sister has done.*]

ERNEST [*blowing slightly through pursed lips*]: Phew! It is hot in here!

FATHER [*bluntly, but amiably*]: Hot! It's non hot! I could do wi' it ten times hotter.

MOTHER: Oh, you! You've got, as I've always said, a hide like a hippopotamus. You ought to have been a salamander.

FATHER: Oh ah, I know tha'll ha'e summat ter say.

MOTHER: Is it raining now, Ernest?

ERNEST: Just a drizzle in the air, like a thick mist.

MOTHER: Ay, isn't it sickening? You'd better take your boots off.

ERNEST [*sitting in his sister's place on the sofa*]: Oh, they're not wet.

MOTHER: They must be damp.

ERNEST: No, they're not. There's a pavement all the way. Here, look at my rose! One of the girls in Coll. gave it me, and the tan-yard girls tried to beg it. They are brazen hussies! 'Gi'e's thy flower, Sorry; gi'e's thy buttonhole' – and one of them tried to snatch it. They have a bobby down by the tan-yard brook every night now. Their talk used to be awful, and it's so dark down there, under the trees. Where's Nellie?

MOTHER: In Coombers'.

ERNEST: Give me a bit of my paper, Father. You know the leaf I want: that with the reviews of books on.

FATHER: Nay, I know nowt about reviews o' books. Here t'art. Ta'e it. [FATHER *hands the newspaper to his son, who takes out two leaves and hands the rest back.*]

ERNEST: Here you are; I only want this.

FATHER: Nay, I non want it. I mun get me washed. We s'll ha'e th' men here directly.

ERNEST: I say, Mater, another seven-and-six up your sleeve?

MOTHER: I'm sure! And in the middle of the term, too! What's it for *this* time?

ERNEST: *Piers the Ploughman*, that piffle, and two books of Horace: Quintus Horatius Flaccus, dear old chap.

MOTHER: And when have you to pay for them?

ERNEST: Well, I've ordered them, and they'll come on Tuesday. I'm sure I don't know what we wanted that Piers Ploughman for – it's sheer rot, and old Beasley could have gassed on it without making us buy it, if he'd liked. Yes, I did feel wild. Seven-and-sixpence!

FATHER: I should non get tem, then. You needna buy 'em unless you like. Dunna get 'em, then.

ERNEST: Well, I've ordered them.

FATHER: If you 'anna the money you canna 'a'e 'em, whether or not.

MOTHER: Don't talk nonsense. If he has to have them, he has. But the money you have to pay for books, and they're no good when you've done with them! – I'm sure it's really sickening, it is!

ERNEST: Oh, never mind, Little; I s'll get 'em for six shillings. Is it a worry, *Mütterchen*?

MOTHER: It is, but I suppose if it has to be, it has.

ERNEST: Old Beasley is an old chough. While he was lecturing this afternoon Arnold and Hinrich were playing nap; and the girls always write letters, and I went fast asleep.

FATHER: So that's what you go'n to Collige for, is it?

ERNEST [*nettled*]: No, it isn't. Only old Beasley's such a dry old ass, with his lectures on Burke. He's a mumbling parson, so what do you expect?

[*The* FATHER *grunts, rises and fetches a clean new bucket from the scullery. He hangs this on the top of the boiler, and turns on the water. Then he pulls off his flannel singlet and stands stripped to the waist, watching the hot water dribble into the bucket. The pail half-filled, he goes out to the scullery on left.*]

Do you know what Professor Staynes said this morning, Mother? He said I'd got an instinct for Latin – and you know he's one of the best fellows in England on the classics: edits Ovid and what-not. An instinct for Latin, he said.

MOTHER [*smiling, gratified*]: Well, it's a funny thing to have an instinct for.

ERNEST: I generally get an alpha plus. That's the highest, you know, Mater. Prof. Staynes generally gives me that.

MOTHER: Your grandfather was always fond of dry reading: economics and history. But I don't know where an instinct for Latin comes from – not from the Lamberts, that's a certainty. Your Aunt Ellen would say, from the Vernons. [*She smiles ironically as she rises to pour him another cup of tea, taking the teapot from the hob and standing it, empty, on the father's plate.*]

ERNEST: Who are the Vernons?

MOTHER [*smiling*]: It's a wonder your Aunt Ellen or your Aunt Eunice has never told you. . . .

ERNEST: Well, they haven't. What is it, *Mütter?*

MOTHER [*sniffing*]: A parcel of nonsense. . . .

ERNEST: Oh, go on, Ma, you are tantalizing! You hug it like any blessed girl.

MOTHER: Yes, your Aunt Ellen always said she would claim the peacock and thistle for her crest, if ever . . .

ERNEST [*delighted*]: The Peacock and Thistle! It sounds like the name of a pub.

MOTHER: My great-great-grandfather married a Lady Vernon – so they say. As if it made any matter – a mere tale!

ERNEST: Is it a fact though, *Matoushka?* Why didn't you tell us before?

MOTHER [*sniffing*]: What should I repeat such –

FATHER [*shouting from the scullery, whence has come the noise of his washing*]: 'An yer put that towil ter dry?

MOTHER [*muttering*]: The towel's dry enough. [*She goes out and is heard taking the roller towel from behind the outer door. She returns, and stands before the fire, holding the towel to dry.* ERNEST LAMBERT, *having frowned and shrugged his shoulders, is reading.*]

MOTHER: I suppose you won't have that bit of rice pudding? [*Her son looks up, reaches over and takes the brown dish from the hearth. He begins to eat from the dish.*]

ERNEST: I went to the 'Savoy' to-day.

MOTHER: I shouldn't go to that vegetable place. I don't believe there's any substance in it.

ERNEST: Substance! Oh, lord! I had an asparagus omelette, I believe they called it; it was too much for me! A great stodgy thing! But I like the Savoy, generally. It was – [*Somebody comes running across the yard.* NELLIE LAMBERT *enters with a rush.*]

NELLIE: Hello! have you done?

FATHER [*from the scullery*]: Are you going to shut that doo-ar! [*Shouting.*]

NELLIE [*with a quick shrug of the shoulders*]: It *is* shut. [*Brightly, to her brother*] Who brought this rose? It'll just do for me. Who gave it you? – Lois?

ERNEST [*flushing*]: What do you want to know for? You're always saying 'Lois'. I don't care a button about Lois.

NELLIE: Keep cool, dear boy, keep cool. [*She goes flying lightly round, clearing the table. The* FATHER, *dripping, bending forward almost double, comes hurrying from the scullery to the fire.* NELLIE *whisks by him, her long pinafore rustling.*]

FATHER [*taking the towel*]: Ow (she) goes rushin' about, draughtin'. [*Rubs his head, sitting on his heels very close to the fire.*]

NELLIE [*smiling contemptuously, to herself*]: Poor kid!

FATHER [*having wiped his face*]: An' there isn't another man in th' kingdom as 'ud stan' i' that scullery stark naked. It's like standin' i' t'cowd watter.

MOTHER [*calmly*]: Many a man stands in a colder.

FATHER [*shortly*]: Ah, I'll back; I'll back there is! Other men's wives brings th' puncheon on to th' 'earthstone, an' gets the watter for 'em, an' –

MOTHER: Other men's wives may do: more fools them: you won't catch me.

FATHER: No, you wunna; you may back your life o' that! An' what if you 'ad to?

MOTHER: Who'd make me?

FATHER [*blustering*]: Me.

MOTHER [*laughing shortly*]: Not half a dozen such.

[*The* FATHER *grunts.* NELLIE, *having cleared the table, pushes him aside a little and lets the crumbs fall into hearth.*]

FATHER: A lazy, idle, stinkin' trick!

[*She whisks the tablecloth away without speaking.*]

An' tha doesna come waftin' in again when I'm washin' me, tha remembers.

ERNEST [*to his mother, who is turning the bread*]: Fancy! Swinburne's dead.

MOTHER: Yes, so I saw. But he was getting on.

FATHER [*to* NELLIE, *who has come to the boiler and is kneeling, getting a lading-can full of water*]: Here, Nellie, gie my back a wash.

[*She goes out, and comes immediately with flannel and soap. She claps the flannel on his back.*]

[*Wincing*] Ooo! The nasty bitch!

[NELLIE *bubbles with laughter. The* MOTHER *turns aside to laugh.*]

NELLIE: You great baby, afraid of a cold flannel! [*She finishes washing his back and goes into the scullery to wash the pots. The* FATHER *takes his flannel shirt from the bookcase cupboard and puts it on, letting it hang over his trousers. Then he takes a little blue-striped cotton bag from his pit trousers' pocket and throws it on the table to his wife.*]

FATHER: Count it. [*He shuffles upstairs.*]

[*The* MOTHER *counts the money, putting it in little piles, checking it from two white papers. She leaves it on the table.* ERNEST *goes into the scullery to wash his hands and is heard talking to his sister, who is wiping the pots. A knock at the outer door.*]

ERNEST: Good evening, Mr Barker.

A VOICE: Good evenin', Ernest.

[*A miner enters: pale, short, but well-made. He has a hard-looking head with short black hair. He lays his cap on a chair.*]

Good evenin', Missis. 'Asn't Carlin come? Mester upstairs?

MOTHER: Yes, he'll be down in a minute. I don't expect Mr Carlin will be many minutes. Sit down, Mr Barker. How's that lad of yours?

BARKER: Well, 'e seems to be goin' on nicely, thank yer. Dixon took th' splints off last wik.

MOTHER: Oh, well, that's better. He'll be alright directly. I should think he doesn't want to go in the pit again.

BARKER: 'E doesna. 'E says 'e shall go farmin' wi' Jakes; but I shanna let 'im. It's nowt o' a sort o' job, that.

MOTHER: No, it isn't. [*Lowering her voice.*] And how's missis?

BARKER [*also lowering his voice*]: Well, I don't know. I want ter get back as soon as I'n got a few groceries an' stuff in. I sent for Mrs Smalley afore I com'n out. An' I'm come an' forgot th' market bag.

MOTHER [*going into the scullery*]: Have mine, have mine. Nay, I've got another. [*Brings him a large carpet bag with leather handles.*]

BARKER: Thank yer, Missis. I can bring it back next wik. You sure you wunna want it?

[*Another knock. Enter another man, fair, pale, smiling, an inconsiderable man.*]

CARLIN: Hgh! Tha's bested me then? Good evenin', Missis.

BARKER: Yes, I'n bet thee.

[*Enter the* FATHER. *He has put on a turn-down collar and a black tie, and his black waistcoat is buttoned, but he wears no coat. The other men take off the large neckerchiefs, grey and white silk, in fine check, and show similar collars. The* FATHER *assumes a slight tone of superiority.*]

FATHER: Well, you've arrived, then! An' 'ow's the missis by now, Joe?

BARKER: Well, I dun know, Walter. It might be any minnit.

FATHER [*sympathetically*]: Hu! We may as well set to, then, an' get it done.

[*They sit at the table, on the side of the fire.* ERNEST LAMBERT *comes in and takes an exercise-book from the shelves and begins to do algebra, using a text-book. He writes with a fountain-pen.*]

CARLIN: They gran' things, them fountain-pens.

BARKER: They are that!

CARLIN: What's th' mak on it, Ernest?

ERNEST: It's an Onoto.

BARKER: Oh-ah! An' 'ow *dun* yer fill it? They says as it hold wi' a vacum.

ERNEST: It's like this: you push this down, put the nib in th' ink, and then pull it out. It's a sort of a pump.

BARKER: Um! It's a canny thing, that!

CARLIN: It is an' a'.

FATHER: Yes, it's a very good idea. [*He is slightly condescending.*]

MOTHER: Look at the bread, Ernest.

ERNEST: Alright, Mater.

> [*She goes upstairs, it being tacitly understood that she shall not know how much money falls to her husband's share as chief 'butty' in the weekly reckoning.*]

BARKER: Is it counted?

FATHER: Yes. It's alright, Ernest?

ERNEST [*not looking up*]: Yes.

> [*They begin to reckon, first putting aside the wages of their day men; then the* FATHER *and* BARKER *take four-and-three-pence, as equivalent to* CARLIN'S *rent, which has been stopped; then the* FATHER *gives a coin each, dividing the money in that way. It is occasionally a puzzling process and needs the Ready Reckoner from the shelf behind.*]

END OF ACT ONE

ACT TWO

Scene, as before: the men are just finishing reckoning.

BARKER *and* CARLIN, *talking in a mutter, put their money in their pockets.* ERNEST LAMBERT *is drawing a circle with a pair of compasses.* CARLIN *rises.*

CARLIN: Well, I might as well be shiftin'.

BARKER: Ay, I mun get off.

[*Enter* NELLIE, *who has finished washing the pots, drying her hands on a small towel. She crosses to the mirror hanging at the right extremity of the mantelpiece.*]

CARLIN: Well, Nellie!

NELLIE [*very amiably, even gaily*]: Good evening, Mr Carlin. Just off?

CARLIN: Yes – ah mun goo.

BARKER: An' 'ow's th' instrument by now, Nellie?

NELLIE: The instrument? Oh, the piano! Ours is a tinny old thing. Oh, yes, you're learning. How are you getting on?

BARKER: Oh, we keep goin' on, like. 'Ave you got any fresh music?

FATHER: Ah, I bet 'er 'as. Ow's gerrin' some iv'ry day or tow.

NELLIE: I've got some Grieg – lovely! Hard, though. It is funny – ever so funny.

BARKER: An' yer iver 'eared that piece 'The Maiden's Prayer'?

NELLIE [*turning aside and laughing*]: Yes. Do you like it? It is pretty, isn't it?

BARKER: I 'ad that for my last piece.

NELLIE: Did you? Can you play it?

BARKER [*with some satisfaction*]: Yes, I can do it pretty fair. 'An yer got th' piece?

NELLIE: Yes. Will you play it for us? Half a minute. [*She finishes stroking her hair up with her side-combs, and, taking the matches from the mantelpiece, leads the way to the door.*] Come on.

FATHER: Yes, step forward, Joe.

[BARKER *goes out after* NELLIE. *Through the open door comes the crashing sound of the miner's banging through* The Maiden's Prayer *on an old sharp-toned piano.* CARLIN *stands listening, and shakes his head at the* FATHER, *who smiles back, glancing at the same time nervously at his son, who has buried his hands in his hair.*]

CARLIN: Well, are ter comin' down, George? [*He moves towards the door.*]

FATHER [*lighting his pipe – between the puffs*]: In about quarter of an hour, Fred.

CARLIN: Good night, then. Good night, Ernest. [*He goes out.*]

[*The* MOTHER *is heard coming downstairs. She glances at her son, and shuts the passage door. Then she hurries to the oven and turns the bread. As she moves away again her husband thrusts out his hand and gives her something.*]

FATHER [*going towards the passage door*]: I know it's a bad wik. [*He goes out.*]

MOTHER [*counts the money he has given her, gives a little rapid clicking with her tongue on the roof of her mouth, tossing her head up once*]: Twenty-eight shillings! [*Counts again.*] Twenty-eight shillings! [*To her son.*] And what was the cheque?

ERNEST [*looking up, with a frown of irritation*]: Eight pounds one and six, and stoppages.

MOTHER: And he gives me a frowsty twenty-eight . . . and I've got his club to pay, and you a pair of boots. . . . Twenty-eight! . . . I wonder if he thinks the house is kept on nothing. . . . I'll take good care he gets nothing extra, I will, too. . . . I knew it, though – I knew he'd been running up a nice score at the Tunns' – that's what it is. There's rent, six-and-six, and clubs seven shillings, besides insurance and gas and everything else. I wonder how he thinks it's done – I wonder if he thinks we live on air?

ERNEST [*looking up with pain and irritation*]: Oh, Mater, don't bother! What's the good? If you worry for ever it won't make it any more.

MOTHER [*softened, conquering her distress*]: Oh, yes, it's all very well for you, but if I didn't worry what would become of us I should like to know?

[GERTIE COOMBER *runs in. She is wearing a large blue felt hat and a Norfolk costume; she is carrying a round basket. From the parlour comes the sound of Grieg's* Anitra's Tanz, *and then* Ase's Tod, *played well, with real sympathy.*]

GERTIE [*with a little shy apprehension*]: Who's in the parlour?

MOTHER: It's only Mr Barker. [*Smiling slightly.*] He wanted to show Nellie how well he could play 'The Maiden's Prayer'.

[GERTIE *suddenly covers her mouth and laughs.*]

GERTIE [*still laughing*]: He, he! I'll bet it was a thump! Pomp! Pomp! [*Makes a piano-thumping gesture.*] Did you hear it, Ernest?

ERNEST [*not looking up*]: Infernal shindy.

[GERTIE *puts up her shoulders and giggles, looking askance at the student who, she knows, is getting tired of interruptions.*]

MOTHER: Yes, I wish he'd go – [*almost whispering*] – and his wife is expecting to go to bed any minute.

[GERTIE *puts her lower lip between her teeth and looks serious. The music stops.* BARKER *and* NELLIE *are heard talking, then the* FATHER. *There is a click of boots on the tiled passage and they enter.*]

NELLIE: What did you think of Mr Barker, Mother? – don't you think it's good? I think it's wonderful – don't you, Ernest?

ERNEST [*grunting*]: Um – it is.

[GERTIE COOMBER *suddenly hides behind her friend and laughs.*]

MOTHER [*to* BARKER]: Yes, I'm sure you get on wonderfully – wonderfully – considering.

BARKER: Yes, ah's non done so bad, I think.

FATHER: Tha 'asna, Joe, tha 'asna, indeed!

MOTHER: Don't forget the bag, Mr Barker – I know you'll want it.

BARKER: Oh, thank yer. Well, I mun goo. Tha'rt comin' down, George?

FATHER: Yes, I'm comin' down, Joe. I'll just get my top-coat on, an' then – [*He struggles awkwardly into his overcoat.*] [BARKER *resumes his grey muffler.*]

BARKER: Well, good night, everybody; good night, Ernest – an' thank yer, Missis.

MOTHER: I hope things will be – [*She nods significantly.*] – alright.

BARKER: Ah, thank yer, I hope it will. I expect so: there's no reason why it shouldn't. Good night.

ALL: Good night, Mr Barker.

[*The* FATHER *and* BARKER *go out. Immediately* NELLIE *flings her arms round* GERTIE'S *neck.*]

NELLIE: Save me, Gert, save me! I thought I was done for that time. . . . I gave myself up! The poor piano! Mother, it'll want tuning now, if it never did before.

MOTHER [*with slight asperity, half-amused*]: It may want at it, then.

GERTIE [*laughing*]: You're done, Nellie, you're done brown! If it's like dropping a saucepan-lid – no – you've got to put up with it!

NELLIE: I don't care. It couldn't be much worse than it is, rotten old thing. [*She pulls off her pinafore and hangs it over the back of a chair, then goes to the mirror, once more to arrange her hair.*]

GERTIE: Oh, come on, Nellie, Cornell's will be crammed.

NELLIE: Don't worry, my dear. What are you going to fetch? Anything nice?

GERTIE: No, I'm not – only bacon and cheese; they send you any stuff: cat and candles – any muck!

[*The* MOTHER *takes the little stool and sits down on it on the hearthrug, lacing up her boots.*]

MOTHER: I suppose you're not going out, Ernest?

ERNEST: No.

MOTHER: Oh – so you can look after the bread. There are two brown loaves at the top; they'll be about half an hour; the white one's nearly done. Put the other in as soon as they come out. Don't go and forget them, now.

ERNEST: No.

MOTHER: He says 'No!' [*She shakes her head at him with indulgent, proud affection.*]

NELLIE [*as if casually, yet at once putting tension into the atmosphere*]: Is Mag coming down?

[*He does not answer immediately.*]

MOTHER: I should think not, a night like this, and all the mud there is.

ERNEST: She said she'd come and do some French. Why?

NELLIE [*with a half-smile, off-handedly*]: Nothing.

MOTHER: You'd never think she'd trapse through all this mud. . . .

NELLIE: Don't bother. She'd come if she had to have water-wings to flop through.

[*GERTIE begins to giggle at the idea. The MOTHER sniffs.*]

ERNEST [*satirically*]: Just as you'd flounder to your Eddie.

[*GERTIE lifts her hands with a little sharp gesture as if to say, 'Now the fun's begun!'*]

NELLIE [*turning suddenly, afire with scorn*]: Oh, should I? You'd catch me running after anybody!

MOTHER [*rising*]: There, that'll do. Why don't you go up town, if you're going?

[*NELLIE LAMBERT haughtily marches off and puts on a dark coat and a blue hat.*]

NELLIE: Is it raining, Gert?

GERTIE: No, it's quite fine.

NELLIE: I'll bet it's fine!

GERTIE: Well, you asked me. It *is* fine; it's not raining.

[*The MOTHER re-enters from the passage, bringing a bonnet and a black coat.*]

NELLIE: Want me to bring anything, Mater?

MOTHER: I shall leave the meat for you.

NELLIE: Alright. Come on, Gert.

[*They go out.*]

MOTHER [*She dreads that her son is angry with her and, affecting carelessness, puts the question to him, to find out*]: Should we be getting a few Christmas-tree things for little Margaret? I expect Emma and Joe will be here for Christmas: it seems nothing but right, and it's only six weeks now.

ERNEST [*coldly*]: Alright.

[*He gets up and takes another book from the shelf without looking at her. She stands a moment suspended in the act of putting a pin through her bonnet.*]

MOTHER: Well, I think we ought to make a bit of Christmas for the little thing, don't you?

ERNEST: Ay. You gave our things to the lads, didn't you? [*He still does not look up from his books.*]

MOTHER [*with a sound of failure in her voice*]: Yes. And they've kept them better than ever I thought they would. They've only broken your blue bird – the one you bought when you were quite little.

[*There is a noise of footsteps and a knock at the door. The* MOTHER *answers.*]

[*Trying to be affable, but diffident, her gorge having risen a little.*] Oh, is it you, Maggie? Come in. How ever have you got down, a night like this? Didn't you get over the ankles in mud? [*She re-enters, followed by a ruddy girl of twenty, a full-bosomed, heavily-built girl, of medium stature and handsome appearance, ruddy and black. She is wearing a crimson tam-o'-shanter and a long grey coat. She keeps her head lowered, and glancing only once splendidly at* ERNEST, *replies with a strange, humble defiance.*]

MAGGIE: No – oh, it's not so bad: besides, I came all round by the road.

MOTHER: I should think you're tired, after school.

MAGGIE: No; it's a relief to walk in the open; and I rather like a black night; you can wrap yourself up in it. Is Nellie out?

MOTHER [*stiffly*]: Yes, she's gone up town.

MAGGIE [*non-significantly*]: Ah, I thought I passed her. I wasn't sure. She wouldn't notice me; it *is* dark over the fields.

MOTHER: Yes, it is. I'm sure *I'm* awful at recognizing people.

MAGGIE: Yes – and so am I, generally. But it's no good bothering. If they like to take offence, they have to. . . . I can't help it.

[*The* MOTHER *sniffs slightly. She goes into the passage and returns with a string net bag. She is ready to go out.*]

MOTHER [*still distantly*]: Won't you take your things off? [*Looks at the bread once more before going.*]

MAGGIE: Ah, thanks, I will. [*She takes off her hat and coat and hangs them in the passage. She is wearing a dark blue cloth 'pinafore-dress', and beneath the blue straps and shoulder pieces a blouse of fine woollen stuff with a small intricate pattern of brown and red. She is flushed and handsome; her features are large, her eyes dark, and her hair falls in loose profusion of black tendrils about her face. The coil at the back is coming undone; it is short and not heavy. She glances supremely at* ERNEST, *feeling him watching her.*]

MOTHER [*at the oven*]: You hear, Ernest? This white cake will be done in about five minutes, and the brown loaves in about twenty.

ERNEST: Alright, my dear.

[*This time it is she who will not look at him.*]

MAGGIE [*laughing a low, short laugh*]: My hair! – is it a sight? I have to keep my coat collar up, or it would drop right down – what bit of it there is. [*She stands away from the mirror, pinning it up; but she cannot refrain from just one glance at herself.*]

[ERNEST LAMBERT *watches her, and then turns to his* MOTHER, *who is pulling on a pair of shabby black gloves.* MRS LAMBERT, *however, keeps her eyes consciously averted; she is offended, and is a woman of fierce pride.*]

MOTHER: Well, I expect I shall see you again, Maggie.

MAGGIE [*with a faint, grave triumph*]: It depends what time you come back. I shan't have to be late.

MOTHER: Oh, you'll be here when I get back.

MAGGIE [*submissive, but with minute irony*]: Very well.

MOTHER: And don't forget that bread, Ernest. [*She picks her bag off the table and goes out, without having looked at either of them.*]

ERNEST [*affectionately*]: No, Little, I won't.

[*There is a pause for a moment.* MAGGIE PEARSON *sits in the arm-chair opposite him, who is on the sofa, and looks straight at him. He raises his head after a moment and smiles at her.*]

MAGGIE: Did you expect me?

ERNEST [*nodding*]: I knew you'd come. You know, when you feel as certain as if you couldn't possibly be mistaken. But I *did* swear when I came out of Coll. and found it raining.

MAGGIE: So did I. Well, not swear, but I was mad. Hasn't it been a horrid week?

ERNEST: Hasn't it? – and I've been so sick of things.

MAGGIE: Of what?

ERNEST: Oh, of fooling about at College – and everything.

MAGGIE [*grimly*]: You'd be sicker of school.

ERNEST: I don't know. At any rate I should be doing something real, whereas, as it is – oh, Coll.'s all foolery and flummery.

MAGGIE: I wish I had a chance of going. I feel as if they'd been pulling things away from me all week – like a baby that has had everything taken from it.

ERNEST [*laughing*]: Well, if school pulls all your playthings and pretty things away from you, College does worse: it makes them all silly and idiotic, and you hate them – and – what then – !

MAGGIE [*seriously*]: Why? How?

ERNEST: Oh, I don't know. You have to fool about so much, and listen when you're not interested, and see old professors like old dogs walking round as large as life with ancient bones they've buried and scratched up again a hundred times; and they're just as proud as ever. It's such a farce! And when you see that farce, you see all the rest: all the waddling tribe of old dogs with their fossil bones – parsons and professors and councillors – wagging their tails and putting their paws on the bones and barking their important old barks – and all the puppies yelping loud applause.

MAGGIE [*accepting him with earnestness*]: Ay! But are they all alike?

ERNEST: Pretty well. It makes you a bit sick. I used to think men in great places were great –

MAGGIE [*fervently*]: I know you did.

ERNEST: – and then to find they're no better than yourself – not a bit –

MAGGIE: Well, I don't see why they should be.

ERNEST [*ignoring her*]: – it takes the wind out of your sails. What's the good of anything if that's a farce?

MAGGIE: What?

ERNEST: The folks at the top. By Jove, if you once lose your illusion of 'great men', you're pretty well disillusioned of everything – religion and everything.

[MAGGIE *sits absorbedly, sadly biting her forefinger: an act which irritates him.*]

[*Suddenly*]: What time did Mother go out?

MAGGIE [*starting*]: I don't know – I never noticed the time.

ERNEST [*rising and going to the oven, picking up the oven-cloth from the hearth*]: At any rate I should think it's five minutes. [*He goes to the oven door, and takes from the lower shelf a 'cake' loaf, baked in a dripping-pan, and, turning it over, taps it with his knuckles.*]

ERNEST: I should think it's done. I'll give it five minutes to soak. [*He puts the bread in the oven shelf, turns the brown loaves, and shuts the oven door. Then he rises and takes a little notebook from the shelf.*]

Guess what I've been doing.

MAGGIE [*rising, dilating, reaching towards him*]: I don't know. What?

ERNEST [*smiling*]: Verses.

MAGGIE [*putting out her hand to him, supplicating*]: Give them to me!

ERNEST [*still smiling*]: They're such piffle.

MAGGIE [*betwixt supplication and command*]: Give them to me.
[*He hands her the little volume, and goes out to the scullery. She sits down and reads with absorption.*
He returns in a moment, his hands dripping with clear water, and, pulling forward the panchion from the corner, takes out the last piece of white dough, scrapes the little pieces together, and begins to work the mass into a flattish ball, passing it from hand to hand. Then he drops the dough into the dripping-pan, and leaves it standing on the hearth. When he rises and looks at her, she looks up at him swiftly, with wide, brown, glowing eyes, her lips parted. He stands a moment smiling down at her.]

ERNEST: Well, do you like them?

MAGGIE [*nodding several times, does not reply for a second*]: Yes, I do.

ERNEST: They're not up to much, though.

MAGGIE [*softly*]: Why not?

ERNEST [*slightly crestfallen at her readiness to accept him again*]: Well, are they?

MAGGIE [*nodding again*]: Yes, they are! What makes you say they're not? I think they're splendid.

ERNEST [*smiling, gratified, but not thinking the same himself*]: Which do you like best?

MAGGIE [*softly and thoughtfully*]: I don't know. I think this is so lovely, this about the almond tree.

ERNEST [*smiling*]: And you under it.

[*She laughs up at him a moment, splendidly.*]
But that's not the best.

MAGGIE [*looking at him expectantly*]: No?

ERNEST: That one, 'A Life History', is the best.

MAGGIE [*wondering*]: Yes?

ERNEST [*smiling*]: It is. It means more. Look how full of significance it is, when you think of it. The profs. would make a great long essay out of the idea. Then the rhythm is finer: it's more complicated.

MAGGIE [*seizing the word to vindicate herself when no vindication is required*]: Yes, it is more complicated: it is more complicated in every way. You see, I didn't understand it at first. It is best. Yes, it is. [*She reads it again.*]

[*He takes the loaf from the oven and puts the fresh one in.*]

ERNEST: What have *you* been doing?

MAGGIE [*faltering, smiling*]: I? Only – only some French.

ERNEST: What, your diary?

MAGGIE [*laughing, confused*]: Ah – but I don't think I want you to see it.

ERNEST: Now, you know you wrote it for me! Don't you think it was a good idea, to get you to write your diary in French? You'd never have done any French at all but for that, and you'd certainly never have told me. . . . You never tell me *your* side.

MAGGIE: There's nothing to tell.

ERNEST [*shaking his finger excitedly*]: That's just what you say, that's just what you say! As many things happen for you as for me.

MAGGIE: Oh, but you go to Derby every day, and you see folks, and I –

ERNEST [*flinging his hand at her*]: Piffle! I tell you – do I tell you the train was late? Do I – ?

MAGGIE [*interrupting, laughing in confusion and humility*]: Yes, you do – ah!

[*He has stopped suddenly with tremendous seriousness and excitement.*]

ERNEST: When?

MAGGIE [*nervous, apologizing, laughing*]: On Sunday – when you told me you'd have –

ERNEST [*flinging her words aside with excited gesture*]: There you are! – you're raking up a trifle to save you from the main issue. Just like a woman! What I said was [*He becomes suddenly slow and fierce.*] you never tell me about you, and you drink me up, get me up like a cup with both hands and drink yourself breathless – and – and there you are – you, you never pour me any wine of yourself –

MAGGIE [*watching him, fascinated and a little bit terror-struck*]: But isn't it your fault?

[*He turns on her with a fierce gesture. She starts.*]

ERNEST: How can it be, when I'm always asking you – ? [*He scratches his head with wild exasperation.*]

MAGGIE [*almost inaudibly*]: Well –

[*He blazes at her so fiercely, she does not continue, but drops her head and looks at her knee, biting her finger.*]

ERNEST [*abruptly*]: Come on – let's see what hundreds of mistakes . . .

[*She looks at him; dilates, laughs nervously, and goes to her coat, returning with a school exercise-book, doubled up. He sits on the sofa, brings her beside him with a swift gesture. Then he looks up at the fire, and starts away round the table.*]

ERNEST [*going into the scullery and crossing the room with dustpan*]: I must mend the fire. There's a book of French verse with my books. Be looking at that while I . . . [*His voice descends to the cellar, where he is heard hammering the coal. He returns directly. She stands at the little cupboard, with her face in a book. She is very short-sighted. He mends the fire without speaking to her, and goes out to wash his hands.*]

ERNEST [*returning*]: Well, what do you think of it? I got it for fourpence.

MAGGIE: I like it ever so much.

ERNEST: You've hardly seen it yet. Come on.

> [*They sit together on the sofa and read from the exercise-book, she nervously.*]

[*Suddenly*]: Now, look here – Oh, the poor verbs! I don't think anybody dare treat them as you do! Look here!

> [*She puts her head closer. He jerks back his head, rubbing his nose frantically, laughing.*]

Your hair did tickle me!

> [*She turns her face to his, laughing, with open mouth. He breaks the spell.*]

Well, have you seen it?

MAGGIE [*hesitating, peering across the lines*]: No-o-o.

ERNEST [*suddenly thrusting his finger before her*]: There! I wonder it doesn't peck your nose off. You *are* a –

> [*She has discovered her mistake and draws back with a little vibrating laugh of shame and conviction.*]

You hussy, what should it have been?

MAGGIE [*hesitating*]: 'Eurent?'

ERNEST [*sitting suddenly erect and startling her up too*]: What! The *preterite*? The *preterite*? And you're talking about going to school!

> [*She laughs at him with nervous shame; when he glares at her, she dilates with fine terror.*]

[*Ominously*]: Well – ?

MAGGIE [*in the depths of laughing despair, very softly and timidly*]: I don't know.

ERNEST [*relaxing into pathetic patience*]: Verbs of motion take *être*, and if you do a thing frequently, use the imperfect. You are – Well, you're inexpressible!

[*They turn to the diary: she covered with humiliation, he aggrieved. They read for a while, he shaking his head when her light springing hair tickles him again.*]

[*Softly*]: What makes you say that?

MAGGIE [*softly*]: What?

ERNEST: That you are 'un enfant de Samedi' – a Saturday child?

MAGGIE [*mistrusting herself so soon*]: Why – it's what they say, you know.

ERNEST [*gently*]: How?

MAGGIE: Oh – when a child is serious; when it doesn't play except on Saturdays, when it is quite free.

ERNEST: And you mean you don't play?

[*She looks at him seriously.*]

No, you haven't got much play in you, have you? – I fool about so much.

MAGGIE [*nodding*]: That's it. You can forget things and play about. I always think of Francis Thompson's *Shelley*, you know – how he made paper boats. . . .

ERNEST [*flattered at the comparison*]: But I don't make paper boats. I tell you, you think too much about me. I tell you I have got nothing but a gift of coloured words. And do I teach you to play? – not to hold everything so serious and earnest? [*He is very serious.*]

[*She nods at him again. He looks back at the paper. It is finished. Then they look at one another, and laugh a little laugh, not of amusement.*]

ERNEST: Ah, your poor diary! [*He speaks very gently.*]

[*She hides her head and is confused.*]

I haven't marked the rest of the mistakes. Never mind – we won't bother, shall we? You'd make them again, just the same.

[*She laughs. They are silent a moment or two; it is very still.*]

You know [*He begins sadly, and she does not answer.*] – you think too much of me – you do, you know.

[*She looks at him with a proud, sceptical smile.*]

[*Suddenly wroth*]: You are such a flat, you won't believe me! But *I* know – if I don't, who does? It's just like a woman, always aching to believe in somebody or other, or something or other.

[*She smiles.*]

I say, what will you have? Baudelaire?

MAGGIE [*not understanding*]: What?

ERNEST: Baudelaire.

MAGGIE [*nervous, faltering*]: But who's – ?

ERNEST: Do you mean to say you don't know who Baudelaire is?

MAGGIE [*defensively*]: How should I?

ERNEST: Why, I gassed to you for half an hour about him, a month back – and now he might be a Maori – !

MAGGIE: It's the names – being foreign.

ERNEST: Baudelaire – Baudelaire – it's no different from Pearson!

MAGGIE [*laughing*]: It sounds a lot better.

ERNEST [*laughing, also, and opening the book*]: Come on! Here, let's have *Maîtresse des Maîtresses*; should we?

MAGGIE [*with gentle persuasiveness*]: Yes. You'll read it?

ERNEST: *You* can have a go, if you like.

[*They both laugh. He begins to read* Le Balcon *in tolerably bad French, but with some genuine feeling. She watches him all the time. At the end, he turns to her in triumph, and she looks back in ecstasy.*]

There! isn't that fine?

[*She nods repeatedly.*]

That's what they can do in France. It's so heavy and full and voluptuous: like oranges falling and rolling a little way along a dark-blue carpet; like twilight outside when the lamp's lighted; you get a sense of rich, heavy things, as if you smelt them, and felt them about you in the dusk: isn't it?

[*She nods again.*]

Ah, let me read you *The Albatross*. This is one of the best – anybody would say so – you see, fine, as good as anything in the world. [*Begins to read.*]

[*There is a light, quick step outside, and a light tap at the door, which opens. They frown at each other, and he whispers.*]

ERNEST: Damn! [*Aloud.*] Hell, Beat!

[*There enters a girl of twenty-three or four; short, slight, pale, with dark circles under her rather large blue eyes, and with dust-coloured hair. She wears a large brown beaver hat and a long grey-green waterproof-coat.*]

BEATRICE WYLD: Hello, Ernest, how are ter? Hello, Mag! Are they all out?

ERNEST [*shutting up the book and drawing away from* MAGGIE. *The action is reciprocal –* BEATRICE WYLD *seats herself in the arm-chair opposite*]: They've gone up town. I don't suppose Nellie will be long.

BEATRICE [*coughing, speaking demurely*]: No, she won't see Eddie to-night.

ERNEST [*leaning back*]: Not till after ten.

BEATRICE [*rather loudly, sitting up*]: What! Does he come round after they shut up shop?

ERNEST [*smiling ironically*]: Ay, if it's getting on for eleven – !

BEATRICE [*turning in her chair*]: Good lawk! – are they that bad? Isn't it fair sickenin'?

ERNEST: He gets a bit wild sometimes.

BEATRICE: I should think so, at that price. Shall you ever get like that, Mag?

MAGGIE: Like what, Beatrice?

BEATRICE: Now, Maggie Pearson, don't pretend to be 'ormin'. She knows as well as I do, doesn't she, Ernest?

MAGGIE: Indeed I don't. [*She is rather high-and-mighty, but not impressive.*]

BEATRICE: Garn! We know you, don't we, Ernie? She's as bad as anybody at the bottom, but she pretends to be mighty 'ormin'.

MAGGIE: I'm sure you're mistaken, Beatrice.

BEATRICE: Not much of it, old girl. We're not often mistaken, are we, Ernie? Get out; we're the 'dead certs' – aren't we, Willie? [*She laughs with mischievous exultance, her tongue between her teeth.*]

MAGGIE [*with great but ineffectual irony*]: Oh, I'm glad somebody is a 'dead cert'. I'm very glad indeed! I shall know where to find one now.

BEATRICE: You will, Maggie.
   [*There is a slight, dangerous pause.*]
BEATRICE [*demurely*]: I met Nellie and Gertie, coming.
ERNEST: Ay, you would.
MAGGIE [*bitterly*]: Oh, yes.
BEATRICE [*still innocently*]: She had got a lovely rose. I won-
   dered –
ERNEST: Yes, she thought Eddie would be peeping over the
   mouse-traps and bird-cages. I bet she examines those
   drowning-mouse engines every time she goes past.
BEATRICE [*with vivacity*]: Not likely, not likely! She marches by
   as if there was nothing but a blank in the atmosphere. You
   watch her. Eyes *Right!* – but she nudges Gert to make her
   see if he's there.
ERNEST [*laughing*]: And then she turns in great surprise.
BEATRICE: No, she doesn't. She keeps 'Eyes Front', and
   smiles like a young pup – and the blushes! – Oh, William,
   too lov'ly f'r anyfing!
ERNEST: I'll bet the dear boy enjoys that blush.
BEATRICE: Ra-ther! [*Artlessly revenant à son mouton.*] And he'll
   have the rose and all, to rejoice the cockles of his heart this
   time.
ERNEST [*trying to ward it off*]: Ay. I suppose you'll see him with
   it on Sunday.
BEATRICE [*still innocently*]: It *was* a beauty, William! Did you
   bring it for her?
ERNEST: I got it in Derby.
BEATRICE [*unmasking*]: Did you? Who *gave* it you, Willie?
ERNEST [*evasively, pretending to laugh*]: Nay, it wouldn't do to
   tell.
BEATRICE: Oh, William, *do* tell us! Was it the Dark, or the
   Athletics?
ERNEST: What if it was neither?
BEATRICE: Oh, Willie, *another!* Oh, it *is* shameful! Think of
   the poor things, what damage you may do them.
ERNEST [*uneasily*]: Yes, they are delicate pieces of goods,
   women. Men have to handle them gently; like a man selling
   millinery.

BEATRICE [*hesitating, then refraining from answering this attack fully*]: It's the hat-pins, Willie dear. But *do* tell us. Was it the Gypsy? – let's see, you generally call it her in German, don't you? – What's the German for gypsy, Maggie? – But was it the Gypsy, or the Athletic Girl that does Botany?

ERNEST [*shaking his head*]: No. It was an Erewhonian.

BEATRICE [*knitting her brows*]: Is that the German for another? Don't say so, William! [*Sighs heavily.*] 'Sigh no more, ladies' – Oh, William! And these two are quite fresh ones, and all. Do you *like* being a mutton-bone, William? – one bitch at one end and one at the other? Do *you* think he's such a juicy bone to squabble for, Maggie?

MAGGIE [*red and mortified*]: I'm sure I don't think anything at all about it, Beatrice.

BEATRICE: No, we've got more sense, we have, Maggie. We know him too well – he's not worth it, is he?

[MAGGIE PEARSON *does not reply.* BEATRICE WYLD *looks at her dress, carefully rubbing off some spot or other; then she resumes.*]

BEATRICE: But surely it's not another, Willie?

ERNEST: What does it matter who it is? Hang me, I've not spoken to – I've hardly said ten words – you said yourself, I've only just known them.

BEATRICE: Oh, Willie, I'm sure I thought it was most desperate – from what you told me.

[*There is another deadly silence.* BEATRICE *resumes innocently, quite unperturbed.*]

Has he told *you*, Maggie?

MAGGIE [*very coldly*]: I'm sure I don't know.

BEATRICE [*simply*]: Oh, he can't have done, then. You'd never have forgot. There's one like a Spaniard – or was it like an Amazon, Willie?

ERNEST: Go on. Either'll do.

BEATRICE: A Spanish Amazon, Maggie – olive-coloured, like the colour of a young clear bit of sea-weed, he said – and, oh, I know! 'great free gestures' – a cool clear colour, not red. Don't you think she'd be lovely?

MAGGIE: I do indeed.

BEATRICE: Too lovely f'r anyfing? – And the other. Oh, yes: 'You should see her run up the college stairs! She can go three at a time, like a hare running uphill.' – And she was top of the Inter. list for Maths and Botany. Don't you wish you were at college, Maggie?

MAGGIE: For some things.

BEATRICE: *I* do. We don't know what he's up to when he's there, do we?

MAGGIE: I don't know that we're so very anxious –

BEATRICE [*convincingly*]: We're not, but he thinks we are, and I believe he makes it all up. I bet the girls just think: 'H'm. Here's a ginger-and-white fellow; let's take a bit of the conceit out of him' – and he thinks they're gone on him, doesn't he?

MAGGIE: Very likely.

BEATRICE: He *does*, Maggie; that's what he does. And I'll bet, if we could hear him – the things he says about us! I'll bet he says there's a girl with great brown eyes –

ERNEST: Shut up, Beat! you little devil – you don't know when to stop.

BEATRICE [*affecting great surprise*]: William! Maggie! Just fancy!!

[*There is another silence, not ominous this time, but charged with suspense.*]

What am I a devil for? [*Half timidly.*]

ERNEST [*flushing up at the sound of her ill-assurance*]: Look here; you may just as well drop it. It's stale, it's flat. It makes no mark, don't flatter yourself – we're sick of it, that's all. It's a case of *ennui*. Vous m'agacez les nerfs. Il faut aller au diable. [*He rises, half laughing, and goes for the dust-pan.*]

BEATRICE [*her nose a trifle out of joint*]: Translate for us, Maggie.

[MAGGIE *shakes her head, without replying. She has a slight advantage now.* ERNEST *crosses the room to go to coal-cellar.* BEATRICE *coughs slightly, adjusts her tone to a casual, dis-interested conversation, and then says, from sheer inability to conquer her spite:*]

You *do* look well, Maggie. I don't think I've seen anybody with such a colour. It's fair fine.

[MAGGIE *laughs and pulls a book towards her. There is silence.* ERNEST'S *steps are heard descending to the cellar and hammering the coal. Presently he re-mounts. The girls are silent,* MAGGIE *pretending to read;* BEATRICE *staring across the room, half smiling, tapping her feet.*]

ERNEST [*hurrying in and putting the coal on the hob*]: Begum, what about the bread?

MAGGIE [*starting up and dilating towards him with her old brilliance*]: Oh, what have we – ? Is it – ? Oh!

[ERNEST *has forestalled her at the oven. There issues a great puff of hot smoke. He draws back a little, and* MAGGIE *utters a quick, tremulous* 'Oh!']

BEATRICE [*with concern*]: Hel-lo, Ernest! that smells a bit thick!

[*He pulls out the loaves one after another. There is one brown loaf much blackened, one in tolerable condition, and the white 'cake' very much scorched on one side.*

BEATRICE *begins to laugh, in spite of her sympathy at the dismay; he is kneeling on the hearth, the oven door open, the oven-cloth in his hand, and the burnt bread toppled out of its tins on the hearth before him.* MAGGIE *is bending over his shoulder, in great concern.* BEATRICE *sputters with more laughter.* ERNEST *looks up at her, and the dismay and chagrin on his face change also to an irresistible troubled amusement at the mishap, and he laughs heartily.* MAGGIE *joins in, strainedly at first, then with natural shaking, and all three laugh with abandonment,* BEATRICE *putting her hand up over her face, and again doubling over till her head touches her knees.*]

ERNEST: No – no! Won't Ma be wild, though! – What a beastly shame!

[BEATRICE *breaks out afresh, and he, though grieved, bubbles again into grudging laughter.*]

Another day and the rotten fire would burn slow, but to-night it's ramped like –

BEATRICE: Hell, Ernie! [*She goes off again into a wild tossing of*

*laughter, hesitating a moment to watch him as he lugubriously picks
up the worst loaf and eyes it over.*]

ERNEST [*grimly*]: It's black bread now, that they talk about.
[*He sniffs the loaf.*]

[BEATRICE *resumes her mad, interrupted laughter.* MAGGIE
sits down on the sofa and laughs till the tears come. ERNEST *taps
the loaf with his finger.*]

BEATRICE: Are you trying to see if it's done, William?
[*From naïve irony she departs into laughter.*]

ERNEST [*answers, his lugubrious soul struggling with laughter, the
girls laughing the while*]: No; I was listening if it sounded
hollow. Hark! [*They listen. Laughter.*] It sounds cindery. I
wonder how deep it goes. [*In a spirit of curiosity, he rises and
fetches a knife, and, pulling a newspaper over the hearth, begins to
cut away the burnt crust. The bread-charcoal falls freely on the
paper. He looks at the loaf.*] By Jove, there *is* a lot! It's like a
sort of fine coke.

[*The girls laugh their final burst, and pant with exhaustion,
their hands pressed in their sides.*]

It's about done for, at any rate. [*Puts it down and takes another
brown loaf; taps it.*] This is not so bad, really, is it? [*Sadly.*] It
sounds a bit desiccated, though. Poor Ma! [*He laughs.*]
She'll say it's your fault, Mag.

MAGGIE [*with astonished, incredulous laughter*]: Me?

BEATRICE: She will, Mag, she will! She'll say if you hadn't
been here making a fuss of him –

MAGGIE [*still laughing*]: I'd better go before she comes.

BEATRICE: You want to scrape that with the nutmeg-grater,
Ernest. Where is it? Here, give it me. [*She takes the loaf, and
ERNEST goes out and returns with the grater. She begins to grate
the loaf.* MAGGIE *takes up the white 'cake' and feels the pale side,
tapping the bottom.*]

MAGGIE [*with decision*]: This isn't done. It's no good cutting
it off till it's all finished. I may as well put it in again.
[*She feels the heat of the two shelves, and puts the loaf on the
upper.*]

[ERNEST *picks up the ruined loaf.*]

ERNEST: What will she say when she sees this?

MAGGIE: Put it on the fire and have done with it.
  [*They look at her in some astonishment at the vandalism of the remark.*]

ERNEST: But . . . [*He looks at the loaf on all sides.*]

MAGGIE: It's no good, and it'll only grieve their poor hearts if they see it. 'What the heart doesn't . . .'

BEATRICE: Ay, put it on, William. What's it matter? Tell 'em the cat ate it.

ERNEST [*hesitating*]: Should I?

BEATRICE [*nudging his elbow*]: Ay, go on.
  [*He puts the loaf on the fire, which is not yet mended, and they stand watching the transparent flames lick it up.*]

ERNEST [*half sad, whimsically, repentant*]: The Staff of Life – !

MAGGIE: It's a faggot now, not a staff.

ERNEST: Ah, well! [*He slides all the cinders and* BEATRICE'S *scrapings together in the newspaper and pours them in the fire.*]

BEATRICE [*holding up her scraped loaf*]: It doesn't show, being brown. You want to wrap it in a damp cloth now. Have you got a cloth?

ERNEST: What? – a clean tea-towel?

BEATRICE: Ay, that'll do. Come here; let's go and wet it.
  [*She goes out, and re-enters directly with the towel screwed up. She folds it round the loaf, the others watching. She sets the shrouded loaf on the table, and they all sit down. There is a little pause.*]
  Have you given over coming down to chapel now, Maggie?

MAGGIE: N-no. I don't know that I have. Why?

BEATRICE: You don't often put in an appearance now.

MAGGIE [*a trifle petulantly*]: Don't I? Well, I don't feel like it, I suppose.

BEATRICE: William, you have something to answer for, my boy. [*She speaks portentously.*]

ERNEST: Shall I? Ne'er mind; I'll say 'adsum' every time. Recording Angel: 'Ernest Lambert.' – 'Adsum!'

BEATRICE: But you don't know what the little Mas say about you, my lad.

ERNEST: The dear little Mas! They will be gossiping about –

BEATRICE [*springing from her chair*]: Look out! there's Nellie. Take that in th' pantry, William. Come out! [*She thrusts the towelled loaf into* ERNEST'S *hands, and he hurries away with it, while she hastily shoots the coal on the fire, and, putting down the dust-pan by the boiler, sits in her chair and looks ""'ormin".'*]

[*Enter* NELLIE LAMBERT *and* GERTIE COOMBER, *blinking.*]

NELLIE [*bending her head to shield her eyes*]: Hasn't Ma come? I never saw her. Hullo, Maggie, you've *not* gone yet, you see. [*She sniffs and goes straight to the oven.*] Goodness, what a smell of burning! Have you been and forgotten the bread? [*She kneels and looks in the oven.*]

BEATRICE [*very quietly and negligently*]: Ernest forgot that one. It's only a bit caught.

[NELLIE *peeps in the panchion where the other loaves are — those baked by the mother.*]

NELLIE: He generally forgets if Maggie's here.

[BEATRICE *bursts out laughing.*]

MAGGIE [*rising, indignant*]: Why, Nellie, when has it ever been burnt before?

NELLIE [*smiling a careless smile*]: Many a time.

MAGGIE: Not when I've been here.

NELLIE: Aren't you going to sit down a bit, Gert?

GERTIE: No, I'm off. Our Frances'll be wanting her ducks. [*She laughs, but does not go.*]

[MAGGIE, *her head hanging, goes to put on her hat and coat. The other girls smile, meaningly, at one another.*]

Are you going, then, Maggie?

MAGGIE [*distantly*]: Yes, it's getting late. I've a long walk, you see.

GERTIE: You have! I'm glad I've not got it. I often wonder how you dare go through those woods on a pitch-dark night.

BEATRICE: I daresn't. [*She laughs at herself.*]

MAGGIE: I'd rather go through our wood than through Nottingham Road, with the people – !

BEATRICE: I'm glad you would, for I wouldn't.

[ERNEST LAMBERT *pulls on his overcoat and his cap. He gathers certain books. He looks at* MAGGIE, *and she at him.*]

MAGGIE: Well, good night, everybody. I shall have to go. [*She hesitates, finding it difficult to break away.*]

BEATRICE AND NELLIE: Good night.

GERTIE: Good night, Maggie, I hope it won't be too muddy for you.

[MAGGIE *laughs slightly.*]

NELLIE [*as the two go through the door, loudly*]: And don't be ever so late back, our Ernest!

[*They do not reply. As their steps are heard passing the wide window,* BEATRICE *flings up her arms and her feet in an ungraceful, exultant glee, flicking her fingers with noiseless venom.*]

BEATRICE [*in an undertone*]: I gave her beans!

NELLIE [*turning, with a smile, and lighting up*]: Did you? What did you say?

GERTIE [*amused, giggling, but shamefaced*]: *Did* you?

BEATRICE [*exultant*]: Oh, lum! I'll bet her cheeks are warm!

END OF ACT TWO

ACT THREE

The same room, half an hour later.

BEATRICE WYLD *sits in the arm-chair, and* NELLIE LAMBERT *on the sofa, the latter doing drawn-thread work on a white tray-cloth, part of which is fixed in a ring: at this part* NELLIE *is stitching.*

BEATRICE: Ah, it makes you grin! the way she used to talk before she had him!

NELLIE: She did. She thought nobody was as good as her Arthur. She's found her mistake out.

BEATRICE: She *has* an' all! He wanted some chips for his supper the other night, when I was there. 'Well,' I said, 'it's not far to Fretwell's, Arthur.' He did look mad at me. 'I'm not going to fetch chips,' he said, a cocky little fool; and he crossed his little legs till I should 'a liked to have smacked his mouth. I said to her, 'Well, Mabel, if *you* do, you're a fool!' – in her state, and all the men that were about! He's not a bit of consideration. You never saw anybody as fagged as she looks.

NELLIE: She does. I felt fair sorry for her when I saw her last Sunday but one. She doesn't look like she used.

BEATRICE: By Jove, she doesn't! He's brought her down a good many pegs. I shouldn't wonder if she wasn't quite safe, either. She told me she had awful shooting pains up her side, and they last for five minutes.

NELLIE [*looking up*]: Oh?

BEATRICE: Ay! I'm glad I'm not in her shoes. They may talk about getting married as they like! Not this child!

NELLIE: Not to a thing like him.

BEATRICE: I asked her if she didn't feel frightened, an' she said she didn't care a scrap. I should care, though – and I'll bet she does, at the bottom.

[*The latch clicks. The* MOTHER *enters, carrying a large net full of purchases, and a brown-paper parcel. She lets these fall heavily on the table, and sits on the nearest chair, panting a little, with evident labour of the heart.*]

MOTHER: Yes, my lady! – you called for that meat, didn't you?

NELLIE [*rising and going to look in the parcels*]: Well, my duck, I looked for you downtown; then when I was coming back, I forgot all about it.

MOTHER: And I – was silly enough – to lug it myself –

NELLIE [*crossing to her mother, all repentant*]: Well, what *did* you for? – you *knew* I could fetch it again! You do do such ridiculous things! [*She begins to take off her mother's bonnet.*]

MOTHER: Yes! We know your fetching it – again. If I hadn't met little Abel Gibson – I really don't think I should have got home.

BEATRICE [*leaning forward*]: If Nellie forgets it, you should forget it, Mrs Lambert. I'm sure you ought not to go lugging all those things.

MOTHER: But I met young Abel Gibson just when I was thinking I should have to drop them – and I said: 'Here, Abel, my lad, are you going home?' and he said he was, so I told him he could carry my bag. He's a nice little lad. He says his father hasn't got much work, poor fellow. I believe that woman's a bad manager. She'd let that child clean up when he got home – and he said his Dad always made the beds. She's not a nice woman, I'm sure. [*She shakes her head and begins to unfasten her coat.*]

[NELLIE, *seeing her mother launched into easy gossip, is at ease on her score, and returns to the bags.*]

You needn't go looking; there's nothing for you.

NELLIE [*petulantly*]: You always used to bring us something –

MOTHER: Ay, I've no doubt I did. . . . [*She sniffs and looks at* BEATRICE WYLD.]

NELLIE [*still looking, unconvinced*]: Hello! Have a grape, Beatrice. [*She offers* BEATRICE *a white-paper bag of very small black grapes.*]

MOTHER: They want washing first, to get the sawdust out. Our Ernest likes those little grapes, and they *are* cheap: only fourpence.

BEATRICE [*looking up from the bag*]: Oh, they are cheap. No, I won't have any, Nellie, thanks.

NELLIE: I'll wash them.

MOTHER: Just let the tap run on them – and get a plate.

NELLIE: Well, as if I shouldn't get a plate! The little Ma thinks we're all daft.

MOTHER [*sniffing – it is her manner of winking*]: Is all the bread done?

NELLIE: Yes. I took the last out about a quarter of an hour ago.

MOTHER [*to* BEATRICE]: Was Maggie Pearson gone when you came?

BEATRICE: No – she's only been gone about three-quarters of an hour.

MOTHER [*tossing her head and lowering her tone confidentially*]: Well, really! I stopped looking at a man selling curtains a bit longer than I should, thinking she'd be gone.

BEATRICE: Pah! – it makes you sick, doesn't it?

MOTHER: It does. You wouldn't think she'd want to come trailing down here in weather like this, would you?

BEATRICE: You wouldn't. I'll bet you'd not catch me! – and she knows what you think, alright.

MOTHER: Of course she does.

BEATRICE: She wouldn't care if the old Dad was here, scowling at her; she'd come.

MOTHER: If that lad was at home.

BEATRICE [*scornfully*]: Ay!

[*The* MOTHER *rises and goes out with her coat.* NELLIE *enters, with a plate of wet black grapes.*]

NELLIE: Now, Beat! [*Offering the grapes.*]

BEATRICE: No, Nellie, I don't think I'll have any.

NELLIE: Go on – have some! Have some – go on! [*Speaks rather imperatively.*]

[BEATRICE *takes a few grapes in her hand.*]
What a scroddy few! Here, have some more.

BEATRICE [*quietly*]: No, Nellie, thanks, I won't have any more. I don't think they'd suit me.

[NELLIE *sits down and begins to eat the grapes, putting the skins on a piece of paper. The* MOTHER *re-enters. She looks very tired. She begins carrying away the little parcels.*]

NELLIE: Don't you put those away, Mother; I'll do it in a minute.

[*The* MOTHER *continues.* NELLIE *rises in a moment or two, frowning.*]

You *are* a persistent little woman! Why don't you wait a bit and let me do it?

MOTHER: Because your father will be in in a minute, and I don't want him peeking and prying into everything, thinking I'm a millionaire. [*She comes and sits down in her rocking-chair by the oven.*]

[NELLIE *continues to carry away the goods, which have littered the table, looking into every parcel.*]

NELLIE: Hello! what are these little things?

MOTHER: Never you mind.

NELLIE: Now, little woman, don't you try to hug yourself and be secretive. What are they?

MOTHER: They're pine-kernels. [*Turning to* BEATRICE.] Our Ernest's always talking about the nut-cakes he gets at Mrs Dacre's; I thought I'd see what they were like. Put them away; don't let him see them. I shan't let him know at all, if they're not up to much. I'm not going to have him saying Mother Dacre's things are better than mine.

BEATRICE: I wouldn't – for I'm sure they're not.

MOTHER: Still, I rather like the idea of nuts. Here, give me one; I'll try it.

[*They each eat a pine-kernel with the air of a connoisseur in flavours.*]

[*Smiling to herself*] Um – aren't they oily!

BEATRICE: They *are*! But I rather like them.

NELLIE: So do I. [*Takes another.*]

MOTHER [*gratified*]: Here, put them away, miss!

[NELLIE *takes another. The* MOTHER *rises and snatches them away from her, really very pleased.*]

There won't be one left, I know, if I leave them with *her*. [*She puts them away.*]

NELLIE [*smiling and nodding her head after her mother; in a whisper*]: Isn't she fussy?

[BEATRICE *puts out her tongue and laughs.*]

MOTHER [*returning*]: I tried a gelatine sponge last week. He likes it much better than cornflower. Mrs Dacre puts them in mincemeat, instead of suet – the pine-kernels. I must try a bit.

BEATRICE: Oh! it *sounds* better.

MOTHER [*seating herself*]: It does. [*She looks down at the bread.*]

[BEATRICE *puts up her shoulders in suspense.*]

I think you let this one dry up.

NELLIE: No, I didn't. It was our Ernest who let it burn.

MOTHER: Trust him! And what's he done? [*She begins to look round.*]

[BEATRICE *pulls a very wry face, straightens it quickly and says calmly:*]

BEATRICE: Is your clock right, Mrs Lambert?

MOTHER [*looking round at the clock*]: Ten minutes – ten minutes fast. Why, what time is it?

BEATRICE: Good lack! [*Rising suddenly.*] It's half-past ten! Won't our Pa rave! 'Yes, my gel – it's turning-out time again. We're going to have a stop put to it.' And our mother will recite! Oh, the recitations! – there's no shutting her up when she begins. But at any rate, she shuts our Pa up, and he's a nuisance when he thinks he's got just cause to be wrath. – Where did I put my things?

MOTHER: I should think that Nellie's put hers on top. [*She looks at* NELLIE.] Don't sit there eating every one of those grapes. You know our Ernest likes them.

NELLIE [*suddenly incensed*]: Good gracious! I don't believe I've had more than half a dozen of the things!

MOTHER [*laughing and scornful*]: Half a dozen!

NELLIE: Yes, half a dozen. – Beatrice, we can't have a thing in this house – everything's for our Ernest.

MOTHER: What a story! What a story! But he *does* like those little grapes.

NELLIE: And everything else.

MOTHER [*quietly, with emphasis*]: He gets a good deal less than you.

NELLIE [*withdrawing from dangerous ground*]: I'll bet.

[GERTIE COOMBER *runs in.*]

BEATRICE: Hello, Gert, haven't you seen John?

GERTIE [*putting up her chin*]: No.

BEATRICE: A little nuisance! – fancy!

GERTIE: Eh, I don't care – not me.

NELLIE: No, it's her fault. She never does want to see him. I wonder any fellow comes to her.

GERTIE [*nonchalantly*]: Um – so do I.

BEATRICE: Get out, Gert; you know you're fretting your heart out 'cause he's not come.

GERTIE [*with great scorn*]: Am I? Oh, *am* I? Not me! If I heard him whistling this moment, I wouldn't go out to him.

NELLIE: Wouldn't you! I'd shove you out, you little cat!

GERTIE [*with great assumption of amusing dignity*]: Oh, would you, indeed!

[*They all laugh.* BEATRICE *pins on her hat before the mirror.*]
You haven't got Ernest to take you home to-night, Beat. Where is he? With Maggie Pearson? Hasn't he come back yet?

MOTHER [*with some bitterness*]: He hasn't. An' he's got to go to college to-morrow. Then he reckons he can get no work done.

GERTIE: Ha! – they're all alike when it suits them.

MOTHER: I should thank her not to come down here messing every Friday and Sunday.

NELLIE: Ah, she's always here. I should be ashamed of *myself*.

BEATRICE: Well – our Pa! I must get off. Good night, everybody. See you to-morrow, Nell.

NELLIE: I'll just come with you across the field. [*She fetches a large white cashmere shawl and puts it over her head. She disposes it round her face at the mirror.* BEATRICE *winks at the* MOTHER.]

GERTIE: She's going to look for Eddie.

NELLIE [*blushing*]: Well, what if I am? Shan't be many minutes, Ma.

MOTHER [*rather coldly*]: I should think not! I don't know what you want at all going out at this time o' night.

> [NELLIE *shrugs her shoulders, and goes out with* BEATRICE WYLD, *who laughs and bids another good night.*]

MOTHER [*when they have gone*]: A silly young hussy, gadding to look for *him*. As if she couldn't sleep without seeing him.

GERTIE: Oh, he always says, 'Come and look for me about eleven.' I bet he's longing to shut that shop up.

MOTHER [*shortly*]: Ha! he's softer than she is, and I'm sure that's not necessary. I can't understand myself how folks can be such looneys. I'm sure I was never like it.

GERTIE: And I'm sure I never should be. I often think, when John's coming, 'Oh, hang it, I wish he'd stay away!'

MOTHER: Ah, but that's too bad, Gertie. If you feel like that you'd better not keep it on any longer. – Yet I used to be about the same myself. *I* was born with too much sense for that sort of slobber.

GERTIE: Yes, isn't it hateful? I often think, 'Oh, get off with you!' I'm sure I should never be like Nellie. – Isn't Ernest late? You'll have Mr Lambert in first.

MOTHER [*bitterly*]: He *is* late. He must have gone every bit of the way.

GERTIE: Nay, I bet he's not – that.

> [*There is silence a moment. The* MOTHER *remembers the bread.*]

MOTHER [*turning round and looking in the panchion*]: Well, there ought to be two more brown loaves. What have they done with them, now? [*Turns over the loaves, and looks about.*]

GERTIE [*laughing*]: I should think they've gone and eaten them, between them.

MOTHER: That's very funny. [*She rises, and is going to look round the room.*]

> [*There is a whistle outside.*]

GERTIE [*turning her head sharply aside*]: Oh, hang it! I'm not going – I'm not!

MOTHER: Who is it? John?

GERTIE: It is, and I'm *not* going.

[*The whistle is heard again.*]

He can shut up, 'cause I'm not going!

MOTHER [*smiling*]: You'll have to just go and speak to him, if he's waiting for you.

[*The whistle is heard louder.*]

GERTIE: Isn't it hateful! I don't care. I'll tell him I was in bed. I should be if my father wasn't at the 'Ram'.

MOTHER [*sighing*]: Ay! But you may guess he's seen Nellie, and she's been saying something to him.

GERTIE: Well, she needn't, then!

[*The whistle goes again.* GERTIE *cannot resist the will of the other, especially as the* MOTHER *bids her go. She flings her hand, and turns with great impatience.*]

He can shut up! What's he want to come at this time for? Oh, *hang* him! [*She goes out slowly and unwillingly, her lips closed angrily. The* MOTHER *smiles, sighs, and looks sad and tired again.*]

MOTHER [*to herself*]: It's a very funny thing! [*She wanders round the room, looking for the bread. She lights a taper and goes into the scullery. Re-passing, she repeats*] A *very* remarkable thing! [*She goes into the pantry on right, and after a moment returns with the loaf in the damp cloth, which she has unfolded. She stands looking at the loaf, repeating a sharp little sound against her palate with her tongue, quickly vibrating her head up and down. To herself.*] So this is it, is it? It's a nice thing! – And they put it down there, thinking I shouldn't see it. It's a nice thing! [*Goes and looks in the oven, then says bitterly*] I always said she was a deep one. And he thinks he'll stop out till his father comes! – And what have they done with the other? – Burnt it, I should think. That's what they've done. It's a nice thing – a nice thing! [*She sits down in the rocking-chair, perfectly rigid, still overdone with weariness and anger and pain.*]

[*After a moment, the garden gate is heard to bang back, and a heavy step comes up the path, halting, punctuated with the scratch and thrust of a walking-stick, rather jarring on the bricked yard.*

The FATHER *enters. He also bends his head a little from the light, peering under his hat-brim.*

The MOTHER *has quickly taken the withered loaf and dropped it in among the others in the panchion.*

The FATHER *does not speak, but goes straight to the passage, and hangs up his hat, overcoat, and jacket, then returns and stands very near the fire, holding his hands close down to the open ruddy grate. He sways slightly when he turns, after a moment or two, and stands with his hands spread behind his back, very near the fire.*

The MOTHER *turns away her head from him.*

He remains thus for a minute or so, then he takes a step forward, and, leaning heavily on the table, begins to pick the grapes from the plate, spitting out the skins into his right hand and flinging them at random towards the fire behind his back, leaning all the time heavily with the left hand on the table.

After a while this irritates the MOTHER *exceedingly.*]

MOTHER: You needn't eat all those grapes. There's somebody else!

FATHER [*speaking with an exaggerated imitation of his son's English*]: 'Somebody else!' Yes, there *is* 'somebody else'! [*He pushes the plate away and the grapes roll on the table.*] I know they was not bought for me! I know it! I know it! [*His voice is rising.*] Somebody else! Yes, there *is* somebody else! I'm not daft! I'm not a fool.

Nothing's got for me. No-o. You can get things for them, you can,

[*The* MOTHER *turns away her head, with a gesture of contempt.*]
[*Continues with maddening tipsy, ironic snarl*] I'm not a fool! I can see it! I can see it! I'm not daft! There's nothing for me, but you begrudge me every bit I put in my mouth.

MOTHER [*with cold contempt*]: You put enough down your own throat. There's no need for anybody else. You take good care you have your share.

FATHER: I have my share. Yes, I do, I do!

MOTHER [*contemptuously*]: Yes, you do.

FATHER: Yes, I do. But I shouldn't if you could help it, you begrudging bitch. What did you put away when I came in, so that I shouldn't see it? Something! Yes! Something you'd got for them! Nobody else. Yes! *I* know you'd got it for somebody else!

MOTHER [*quietly, with bitter scorn*]: As it happens, it was nothing.

FATHER [*his accent is becoming still more urban. His O's are A's, so that 'nothing' is 'nathing'*]: Nathing! Nathing! You're a liar, you're a liar. I heard the scuffle. You don't think I'm a fool, do you, woman?

[*She curls her lips in a deadly smile.*]

FATHER: I know, I know! Do *you* have what you give me for dinner? No, you don't. You take good care of it!

MOTHER: Look here, you get your good share. Don't think *you* keep the house. Do you think I manage on the few lousy shillings you give me? No, you get as much as you deserve, if any man did. And if *you* had a rice pudding, it was because *we* had *none*. Don't come here talking. *You* look after *yourself*, there's no mistake.

FATHER: An' I mean to, an' I mean to!

MOTHER: Very well, then!

FATHER [*suddenly flaring*]: But I'm not going to be treated like a dog in my own house! I'm *not*, so don't think it! I'm master in this house, an' I'm *going* to be. I tell you, I'm master of this house.

MOTHER: You're the only one who thinks so.

FATHER: I'll stop it! I'll put a stop to it. They can go – they can go!

MOTHER: You'd be on short commons if they did.

FATHER: What? What? Me! You saucy bitch, I can keep myself, an' you as well, an' him an' all as holds his head above me – am doing – an' I'll stop it, I'll stop it – or they can go.

MOTHER: Don't make any mistake – *you* don't keep us. You hardly keep yourself.

FATHER: Do I? – do I? And who does keep 'em, then?

MOTHER: I do – and the girl.

FATHER: You do, do you, you snappy little bitch! You do, do you? Well, keep 'em yourself, then. Keep that lad in his idleness yourself, then.

MOTHER: Very willingly, very willingly. And that lad works ten times as hard as you do.

FATHER: Does he? I should like to see him go down th' pit every day! I should like to see him working every day in th' hole. No, he won't dirty his fingers.

MOTHER: Yes, you wanted to drag all the lads into the pit, and you only begrudge them because I wouldn't let them.

FATHER [*shouting*]: You're a liar – you're a liar! I never wanted 'em in th' pit.

MOTHER [*interrupting*]: You did your best to get the other two there, anyway.

FATHER [*still shouting*]: You're a liar – I never did anything of the sort. What other man would keep his sons doing nothing till they're twenty-two? Where would you find another? Not that I begrudge it him – I don't, bless him. . . .

MOTHER: Sounds like it.

FATHER: I don't. I begrudge 'em nothing. I'm willing to do everything I can for 'em, and 'ow do they treat me? Like a dog, I say, like a dog!

MOTHER: And whose fault is it?

FATHER: Yours, you stinking hussy! It's you as makes 'em like it. They're like you. You teach 'em to hate me. You make me like dirt for 'em: you set 'em against me . . .

MOTHER: You set them yourself.

FATHER [*shouting*]: You're a liar! [*He jumps from his chair and stands bending towards her, his fist clenched and ready and threatening.*] It's you. It always 'as been you. You've done it –
[*Enter* ERNEST LAMBERT.]

ERNEST [*pulling off his cap and flashing with anger*]: It's a fine row you're kicking up. I should bring the neighbours in!

FATHER: I don't care a damn what I do, you sneering devil, you! [*He turns to his son, but remains in the same crouching, threatening attitude.*]

ERNEST [*flaring*]: You needn't swear at me, either.

FATHER: I shall swear at who the devil I like. Who are you, you young hound – who are you, you measley little –

ERNEST: At any rate, I'm not a foul-mouthed drunken fool.

FATHER [*springing towards him*]: What! I'll smite you to the ground if you say it again, I will, I *will*!

ERNEST: Pah! [*He turns his face aside in contempt from the fist brandished near his mouth.*]

FATHER [*shouting*]: What! Say it! I'll drive my fist through you!

ERNEST [*suddenly tightening with rage as the fist is pushed near his face*]: Get away, you spitting old fool!

[*The* FATHER *jerks nearer and trembles his fist so near the other's nose that he draws his head back, quivering with intense passion and loathing, and lifts his hands.*]

MOTHER: Ernest, Ernest, don't!

[*There is a slight relaxation.*]

[*Lamentable, pleading*]: Don't say any more, Ernest! Let him say what he likes. What should I do if . . .

[*There is a pause.*

ERNEST *continues rigidly to glare into space beyond his father. The* FATHER *turns to the* MOTHER *with a snarling movement, which is nevertheless a movement of defeat. He withdraws, sits down in the arm-chair, and begins, fumbling, to get off his collar and tie, and afterwards his boots.*

ERNEST *has taken a book, and stands quite motionless, looking at it. There is heard only the slash of the* FATHER'S *boot-laces. Then he drags off the boot, and it falls with a loud noise.*

ERNEST, *very tense, puts down the book, takes off his overcoat, hangs it up, and returns to the side of the sofa nearest the door, where he sits, pretending to read.*

There is silence for some moments, and again the whip of boot-laces. Suddenly a snarl breaks the silence.]

FATHER: But don't think I'm going to be put down in my own house! It would take a better man than you, you white-faced jockey – or your mother either – or all the lot of you put together! [*He waits awhile.*] I'm not daft – I can see what she's driving at. [*Silence.*] I'm not a fool, if you think so. I can pay you yet, you sliving bitch! [*He sticks out his chin at his wife.*]

[ERNEST *lifts his head and looks at him.*]

[*Turns with renewing ferocity on his son*] Yes, and you either.

I'll stand no more of your chelp. I'll stand no *more*! Do you hear me?

MOTHER: Ernest!

[ERNEST *looks down at his book. The* FATHER *turns to the* MOTHER.]

FATHER: Ernest! Ay, prompt him! Set him on – you know how to do it – you know how to do it!

[*There is a persistent silence.*]

I know it! I know it! I'm not daft, I'm not a fool! [*The other boot falls to the floor. He rises, pulling himself up with the arms of the chair, and, turning round, takes a Waterbury watch with a brass chain from the wall beside the bookcase: his pit watch that the* MOTHER *hung there when she put his pit-trousers in the cupboard – and winds it up, swaying on his feet as he does so. Then he puts it back on the nail, and a key swings at the end of the chain. Then he takes a silver watch from his pocket, and, fumbling, missing the keyhole, winds that up also with a key, and, swaying forward, hangs it up over the cupboard. Then he lurches round, and, limping pitiably, goes off upstairs.*

There is a heavy silence. The Waterbury watch can be heard ticking.]

ERNEST: I would kill him, if it weren't that I shiver at the thought of touching him.

MOTHER: Oh, you mustn't! Think how awful it would be if there were anything like that. I couldn't bear it.

ERNEST: He is a damned, accursed fool!

[*The* MOTHER *sighs.* ERNEST *begins to read. There is a quick patter of feet, and* GERTIE COOMBER *comes running in.*]

GERTIE: Has Mr Lambert come?

MOTHER: Ay – in bed.

GERTIE: My father hasn't come yet. Isn't it sickening?

MOTHER: It is, child. They want horsewhipping, and those that serve them, more.

GERTIE: I'm sure we haven't a bit of peace of our lives. I'm sure when Mother was alive, she used to say her life was a burden, for she never knew when he'd come home, or how.

MOTHER: And it is so.

GERTIE: Did you go far, Ernest?

ERNEST [*not looking up*]: I don't know. Middling.

71

MOTHER: He must have gone about home, for he's not been back many minutes.

GERTIE: There's our Frances shouting!
[*She runs off.*]

MOTHER [*quietly*]: What did you do with that other loaf?

ERNEST [*looking up, smiling*]: Why, we forgot it, and it got all burned.

MOTHER [*rather bitterly*]: Of course you forgot it. And where is it?

ERNEST: Well, it was no good keeping it. I thought it would only grieve your heart, the sight of it, so I put it on the fire.

MOTHER: Yes, I'm sure! That was a nice thing to do, I must say! . . . Put a brown loaf on the fire, and dry the only other one up to a cinder!
[*The smile dies from his face, and he begins to frown.*]
[*She speaks bitterly*] It's always alike, though. If Maggie Pearson's here, nobody else matters. It's only a laughing matter if the bread gets burnt to cinders and put on the fire. [*Suddenly bursts into a glow of bitterness.*] It's all very well, my son – you may talk about caring for me, but when it comes to Maggie Pearson it's very little you care for me – or Nellie – or anybody else.

ERNEST [*dashing his fingers through his hair*]: You talk *just* like a woman! As if it makes any difference! As if it makes the least difference!

MOTHER [*folding her hands in her lap and turning her face from him*]: Yes, it does.

ERNEST [*frowning fiercely*]: It doesn't. Why should it? If I like apples, does it mean I don't like – bread? You know, Ma, it doesn't make any difference.

MOTHER [*doggedly*]: *I* know it does.

ERNEST [*shaking his finger at her*]: But why should it, why should it? You know you wouldn't be interested in the things we talk about: you know you wouldn't.

MOTHER: Why shouldn't I?

ERNEST: Should you, now? Look here: we talked about French poetry. Should you care about that?
[*No answer.*]

You know you wouldn't! And then we talked about those pictures at the Exhibition – about Frank Brangwyn – about Impressionism – for ever such a long time. You would only be bored by that –

MOTHER: Why should I? You never tried.

ERNEST: But you wouldn't. You wouldn't care whether it's Impressionism or pre-Raphaelism. [*Pathetically*.]

MOTHER: I don't see why I shouldn't.

ERNEST [*ruffling his hair in despair; after a pause*]: And, besides, there are lots of things you can't talk to your own folks about, that you would tell a stranger.

MOTHER [*bitterly*]: Yes, I know there are.

ERNEST [*wildly*]: Well, I can't help it – can I, now?

MOTHER [*reluctantly*]: No – I suppose not – if you say so.

ERNEST: But you know – !

MOTHER [*turning aside again; with some bitterness and passion*]: I do know, my boy – I *do* know!

ERNEST: But I can't help it.

[*His* MOTHER *does not reply, but sits with her face averted.*] Can I, now? Can I?

MOTHER: You say not.

ERNEST [*changing the position again*]: And you wouldn't care if it was Alice, or Lois, or Louie. You never row me if I'm a bit late when I've been with them. . . . It's just Maggie, because you don't like her.

MOTHER [*with emphasis*]: No, I *don't* like her – and I *can't* say I do.

ERNEST: But why not? Why not? She's as good as I am – and I'm sure you've nothing against her – have you, now?

MOTHER [*shortly*]: No, I don't know I've anything against her.

ERNEST: Well, then, what do you get so wild about?

MOTHER: Because I don't like her, and I never shall, so there, my boy!

ERNEST: Because you've made up your mind not to.

MOTHER: Very well, then.

ERNEST [*bitterly*]: And you did from the beginning, just because she happened to care for me.

MOTHER [*with coldness*]: And does nobody else care for you, then, but her?

ERNEST [*knitting his brows and shaking his hands in despair*]: Oh, but it's not a question of that.

MOTHER [*calmly, coldly*]: But it is a question of that.

ERNEST [*fiercely*]: It isn't! You know it isn't! I care just as much for you as ever – you know I do.

MOTHER: It looks like it, when night after night you leave me sitting up here till nearly eleven – and gone eleven sometimes –

ERNEST: Once, Mother, once – and that was when it was her birthday.

MOTHER [*turning to him with the anger of love*]: And how many times is it a quarter to eleven, and twenty to?

ERNEST: But you'd sit up just the same if I were in; you'd sit up reading – you know you would.

MOTHER: You don't come in to see.

ERNEST: When I am in, do you go to bed before then?

MOTHER: I do.

ERNEST: Did you on Wednesday night, or on Tuesday, or on Monday?

MOTHER: No; because you were working.

ERNEST: I was *in*.

MOTHER: I'm not going to go to bed and leave you sitting up, and I'm not going to go to bed to leave you to come in when you like . . . so there!

ERNEST [*beginning to unfasten his boots*]: Alright – I can't help it, then.

MOTHER: You mean you won't.

[*There is a pause.* ERNEST *hangs his head, forgetting to unlace his boot further.*]

ERNEST [*pathetically*]: You don't worry our Nellie. Look, she's out now. You never row her.

MOTHER: I do. I'm always telling her.

ERNEST: Not like this.

MOTHER: I do! I called her all the names I could lay my tongue to last night.

ERNEST: But you're not nasty every time she goes out to

see Eddie, and you don't for ever say nasty things about
him. . . .

[*There is a moment of silence, while he waits for an answer.*]

ERNEST: And I always know you'll be sitting here working
yourself into a state if I happen to go up to Herod's Farm.

MOTHER: Do I? – and perhaps you would, if you sat here
waiting all night –

ERNEST: But, Ma, you don't care if Nellie's out.

MOTHER [*after brooding awhile; with passion*]: No, my boy, because she doesn't mean the same to me. She has never
understood – she has not been – like you. And now – you
seem to care nothing – you care for *anything* more than
home: you tell me nothing but the little things: you used to
tell me everything; you used to come to me with everything; but now – I don't *do* for you now. You have to find
somebody else.

ERNEST: But I can't help it. I can't help it. I have to grow
up – and things are different to us now.

MOTHER [*bitterly*]: Yes, things *are* different to us now. They
never used to be. And you say I've never tried to care for
her. I have – I've tried and tried to like her, but I can't, and
it's no good.

ERNEST [*pathetically*]: Well, my dear, we shall have to let it be,
then, and things will have to go their way. [*He speaks with
difficulty.*] You know, Mater – I don't care for her – really –
not half as I care for you. Only, just now – well, I can't
help it, I can't help it. But I care just the same – for you –
I do.

MOTHER [*turning with a little cry*]: But I thought you didn't!
[*He takes her in his arms, and she kisses him, and he hides
his face in her shoulder. She holds him closely for a moment;
then she kisses him and gently releases him. He kisses her. She
gently draws away, saying, very tenderly*]
There! – Nellie will be coming in.

ERNEST [*after a pause*]: And you do understand, don't you,
Mater?

MOTHER [*with great gentleness, having decided not to torment him*]:
Yes, I understand now. [*She bluffs him.*]

[ERNEST *takes her hand and strokes it a moment. Then he bends down and continues to unfasten his boots. It is very silent.*]

I'm sure that hussy ought to be in – just look at the time!

ERNEST: Ay, it's scandalous!

[*There are in each of their voices traces of the recent anguish, which makes their speech utterly insignificant. Nevertheless, in thus speaking, each reassures the other that the moment of abnormal emotion and proximity is passed, and the usual position of careless intimacy is reassumed.*]

MOTHER [*rising*]: I shall have to go and call her – a brazen baggage!

[*There is a rattle of the yard gate, and* NELLIE *runs in, blinking very much.*]

NELLIE [*out of breath; but very casually*]: Hello, our Ernest, you home?

MOTHER: Yes, miss, and been home long ago. I'll not have it, my lady, so you needn't think it. You're not going to be down there till this time of night! It's disgraceful. What will his mother say, do you think, when he walks in at past eleven?

NELLIE: She can say what she likes. Besides, she'll be in bed.

MOTHER: She'll hear him, for all that. I'd be ashamed of myself, that I would, standing out there slobbering till this time of night! I don't know how anyone can be such a fool!

NELLIE [*smiling*]: Perhaps not, my dear.

MOTHER [*slightly stung*]: No, and I should be sorry. I don't know what he wants running up at this time of a night.

NELLIE: Oh, Mother, don't go on again! We've heard it a dozen times.

MOTHER: And you'll hear it two dozen.

[ERNEST, *having got off his shoes, begins to take off his collar and tie.* NELLIE *sits down in the arm-chair.*]

NELLIE [*dragging up the stool and beginning to unlace her boots*]: I could hear my father carrying on again. Was he a nuisance?

MOTHER: Is he ever anything else when he's like that?

NELLIE: He *is* a nuisance. I wish he was far enough! Eddie could hear every word he said.

ERNEST: Shame! Shame!

NELLIE [*in great disgust*]: It is! *He* never hears anything like that. Oh, I was wild. I could have killed him!

MOTHER: You should have sent him home; then he'd not have heard it at all.

NELLIE: He'd only just come, so I'm sure I wasn't going to send him home then.

ERNEST: So you heard it all, to the mild-and-bitter end?

NELLIE: No, I didn't. And I felt such a fool!

ERNEST: You should choose your spot out of earshot, not just by the garden gate. What did you do?

NELLIE: I said, 'Come on, Eddie, let's get away from this lot.' I'm sure I shouldn't have wondered if he'd gone home and never come near again.

MOTHER [*satirically*]: What for?

NELLIE: Why – when he heard that row.

MOTHER: I'm sure it was very bad for him, poor boy.

NELLIE [*fiercely*]: How should you like it?

MOTHER: I shouldn't have a fellow there at that time at all.

ERNEST: You thought a father-in-law that kicked up a shindy was enough to scare him off, did you? Well, if you choose your girl, you can't choose your father-in-law – you'll have to tell him that.

[NELLIE *has taken off her shoes. She stands in front of the mirror and uncoils her hair, and plaits it in a thick plait which hangs down her back.*]

MOTHER: Come, Ernest; you'll never want to get up in the morning.

NELLIE [*suddenly*]: Oh! There now! I never gave him that rose.

[*She looks down at her bosom and lifts the head of a rather crushed rose.*] What a nuisance!

ERNEST: The sad history of a rose between two hearts:

> 'Rose, red rose, that burns with a low flame,
>   What has broken you?
> Hearts, two hearts caught up in a game
>   Of shuttlecock – Amen!'

NELLIE [*blushing*]: Go on, you soft creature! [*Looks at the rose.*]

ERNEST: Weep over it.

NELLIE: Shan't!

ERNEST: And pickle it, like German girls do.

NELLIE: Don't be such a donkey.

ERNEST: Interesting item: final fate of the rose.

[NELLIE *goes out; returns in a moment with the rose in an egg-cup in one hand, and a candle in the other. The* MOTHER *rises.*]

ERNEST: I'll rake, Mother.

[NELLIE *lights her candle, takes her shawl off the table, kisses her mother good night, and bids her brother good night as he goes out to the cellar.*

The MOTHER *goes about taking off the heavy green table-cloth, disclosing the mahogany, and laying a doubled table-cloth half across. She sets the table with a cup and saucer, plate, knife, sugar-basin, brown-and-white teapot and tea-caddy. Then she fetches a tin bottle and a soiled snapbag, and lays them together on the bare half of the table. She puts out the salt and goes and drags the pit-trousers from the cupboard and puts them near the fire.*

Meanwhile ERNEST *has come from the cellar with a large lump of coal, which he pushes down in the fireplace so that it shall not lodge and go out.*]

MOTHER: You'll want some small bits. – And bring a few pieces for him in the morning.

ERNEST [*returning to the cellar with the dust-pan*]: Alright! I'll turn the gas out now.

[*The* MOTHER *fetches another candle and continues her little tasks. The gas goes suddenly down and dies slowly out.*

ERNEST *comes up with his candlestick on a shovelful of coal. He puts the candle on the table, and puts some coal on the fire, round the 'raker'. The rest he puts in the shovel on the hearth. Then he goes to wash his hands.*

The MOTHER, *leaving her candle in the scullery, comes in with an old iron fire-screen which she hangs on the bars of the grate, and the ruddy light shows over and through the worn iron top.*

ERNEST *is heard jerking the roller-towel. He enters, and goes to his mother, kissing her forehead, and then her cheek, stroking her cheek with his finger-tips.*]

ACT THREE

ERNEST: Good night, my dear.

MOTHER: Good night. – Don't you want a candle?

ERNEST: No – blow it out. Good night.

MOTHER [*very softly*]: Good night.

[*There is in their tones a dangerous gentleness – so much gentleness that the safe reserve of their souls is broken.*

ERNEST *goes upstairs. His bedroom door is heard to shut.*

The MOTHER *stands and looks in the fire. The room is lighted by the red glow only. Then in a moment or two she goes into the scullery, and after a minute – during which running of water is heard – she returns with her candle, looking little and bowed and pathetic, and crosses the room, softly closing the passage door behind her.*]

END OF ACT THREE

THE DAUGHTER-IN-LAW

A PLAY IN FOUR ACTS
(1912)

CHARACTERS

MRS GASCOIGNE
JOE
MRS PURDY
MINNIE
LUTHER
CABMAN

The action of the play takes place in the kitchen of Luther Gascoigne's new home.

ACT ONE

SCENE I

A collier's kitchen – not poor. Windsor chairs, deal table, dresser of painted wood, sofa covered with red cotton stuff. Time: About half-past two of a winter's afternoon.

A large, stoutish woman of sixty-five, with smooth black hair parted down the middle of her head: MRS GASCOIGNE.

Enter a young man, about twenty-six, dark, good-looking; has his right arm in a sling; does not take off cap: JOE GASCOIGNE.

MRS GASCOIGNE: Well, I s'd ha' thought thy belly 'ud a browt thee whoam afore this.

[JOE *sits on sofa without answering.*]

Doesn't ter want no dinner?

JOE [*looking up*]: I want it if the' is ony.

MRS GASCOIGNE: An' if the' isna, tha can go be out? Tha talks large, my fine jockey! [*She puts a newspaper on the table; on it a plate and his dinner.*] Wheer dost reckon ter's bin?

JOE: I've bin ter th' office for my munny.

MRS GASCOIGNE: Tha's niver bin a' this while at th' office.

JOE: They kep' me ower an hour, an' then gen me nowt.

MRS GASCOIGNE: Gen thee nowt! Why, how do they ma'e that out? It's a wik sin' tha got hurt, an' if a man wi' a broken arm canna ha' his fourteen shillin' a week accident pay, who can, I s'd like to know?

JOE: They'll gie me nowt, whether or not.

MRS GASCOIGNE: An' for why, prithee?

JOE [*does not answer for some time; then, suddenly*]: They reckon I niver got it while I wor at work.

MRS GASCOIGNE: Then where did ter get it, might I ax? I'd think they'd like to lay it onto me.

JOE: Tha talks like a fool, Mother.

MRS GASCOIGNE: Tha looks like one, me lad. [*She has given*

83

him his dinner; he begins to eat with a fork.] Here, hutch up,
gammy-leg – gammy-arm.

[*He makes room; she sits by him on the sofa and cuts up his
meat for him.*]

It's a rum un as I should start ha'in' babies again, an'
feedin' 'em wi' spoon-meat. [*Gives him a spoon.*] An' now
let's hear why they winna gi'e thee thy pay. Another o'
Macintyre's dirty knivey dodges, I s'd think.

JOE: They reckon I did it wi' foolery, an' not wi' work.

MRS GASCOIGNE: Oh indeed! An' what by that?

JOE [*eating*]: They wunna gie me nowt, that's a'.

MRS GASCOIGNE: It's a nice thing! An' what did ter say?

JOE: I said nowt.

MRS GASCOIGNE: Tha wouldna'! Tha stood like a stuffed
duck, an' said thank-yer.

JOE: Well, it wor raight.

MRS GASCOIGNE: How raight?

JOE: I did do it wi' foolery.

MRS GASCOIGNE: Then what did ter go axin' fer pay fer?

JOE: I did it at work, didna I? An' a man as gets accident at
work's titled ter disability pay, isna he?

MRS GASCOIGNE: Tha said a minnit sin' as tha got it wi'
foolery.

JOE: An' so I did.

MRS GASCOIGNE: I niver 'eered such talk i' my life.

JOE: I dunna care what ter's 'eered an' what t'asna. I wor
foolin' wi' a wringer an' a pick-heft – ta's it as ter's a mind.

MRS GASCOIGNE: What, down pit?

JOE: I' th' stall, at snap time.

MRS GASCOIGNE: Showin' off a bit, like?

JOE: Ye'.

MRS GASCOIGNE: An' what then?

JOE: Th' wringer gen me a rap ower th'arm, an' that's a'.

MRS GASCOIGNE: An' tha reported it as a accident?

JOE: It wor accident, worn't it? I niver did it a'purpose.

MRS GASCOIGNE: But a pit accident.

JOE: Well, an' what else wor't? It wor a h'accident I got i' th'
pit, i' th' sta' wheer I wor workin'.

MRS GASCOIGNE: But not *while* tha wor workin'.

JOE: What by that? – it wor a pit accident as I got i' th' stall.

MRS GASCOIGNE: But tha didna tell 'em how it happened.

JOE: I said some stuff fell on my arm, an' brok' it. An' worna that trew?

MRS GASCOIGNE: It wor very likely trew enough, lad, if on'y they'd ha' believed it.

JOE: An they would ha' believed it, but for Hewett bully-raggin' Bettesworth 'cos he knowed he was a chappil man. [*He imitates the underground manager, Hewett, and Bettesworth, a butty.*] 'About this accident, Bettesworth. How exactly did it occur?' 'I couldn't exactly say for certing, sir, because I wasn't linkin'.' 'Then tell me as near as you can.' 'Well, Mester, I'm sure I don't know.' 'That's curious, Bettesworth – I must have a report. Do you know anything about it, or don't you? It happened in your stall; you're responsible for it, and I'm responsible for you.' 'Well, Gaffer, what's right's right, I suppose, ter th' mesters or th' men. An' 'e wor conjurin' a' snap-time wi' a pick-heft an' a wringer, an' the wringer catched 'im ower th' arm.' 'I thought you didn't know!' 'I said *for certain* – I didn't see exactly how 'twas done.'

MRS GASCOIGNE: Hm.

JOE: Bettesworth 'ud non ha' clat-fasted but for nosy Hewett. He says, 'Yo know, Joseph, when he says to me, "Do you know anything about that haccident?" – then I says to myself, "Take not the word of truth hutterly outer thy mouth."'

MRS GASCOIGNE: If he took a bit o' slaver outen's mouth, it 'ud do.

JOE: So this mornin' when I went ter th' office, Mester Salmon he com out an' said: "Ow did this haccident occur, Joseph?' and I said, 'Some stuff fell on't.' So he says, 'Stuff fell on't, stuff fell on't! You mean coal or rock or what?' So I says, 'Well, it worn't a thipenny bit.' 'No,' he says, 'but what was it?' 'It wor a piece o' clunch,' I says. 'You don't use clunch for wringers,' he says, 'do you?' 'The wringin' of the nose bringeth forth blood,' I says –

MRS GASCOIGNE: Why, you know you never did. [*She begins making a pudding.*]

JOE: No – b'r I'd ha' meant t'r'a done.

MRS GASCOIGNE: We know thee! Tha's done thysen one i' th' eye this time. When dost think tha'll iver get ter be a butty, at this rate? There's Luther nowt b'r a day man yet.

JOE: I'd as lief be a day man as a butty, i' pits that rat-gnawed there's hardly a stall worth havin'; an' a company as 'ud like yer ter scrape yer tabs afore you went home, for fear you took a grain o' coal.

MRS GASCOIGNE: Maybe – but tha's got ter get thy livin' by 'em.

JOE: I hanna. I s'll go to Australia.

MRS GASCOIGNE: Tha'lt do no such thing, while I'm o' this earth.

JOE: Ah, but though, I shall – else get married, like our Luther.

MRS GASCOIGNE: A fat sight better off tha'lt be for that.

JOE: You niver know, Mother, dun yer?

MRS GASCOIGNE: You dunna, me lad – not till yer find yerself let in. Marriage is like a mouse-trap, for either man or woman. You've soon come to th' end o' th' cheese.

JOE: Well, ha'ef a loaf's better nor no bread.

MRS GASCOIGNE: Why, wheer's th' loaf as tha'd like ter gnawg a' thy life?

JOE: Nay, nowhere yet.

MRS GASCOIGNE: Well, dunna thee talk, then. Tha's done thysen harm enow for one day, wi' thy tongue.

JOE: An' good as well, Mother – I've aten my dinner, a'most.

MRS GASCOIGNE: An' swilled thy belly afore that, methinks.

JOE: Niver i' this world!

MRS GASCOIGNE: And I've got thee to keep on ten shillin's a wik club-money, han I?

JOE: Tha needna, if ter doesna want. Besides, we s'll be out on strike afore we know wheer we are.

MRS GASCOIGNE: I'm sure. You've on'y bin in –

JOE: Now, Mother, spit on thy hands an' ta'e fresh hold. We s'll be out on strike in a wik or a fortnit –

MRS GASCOIGNE: Strike's a' they're fit for – a pack o' slutherers as ... [*Her words tail off as she goes into pantry.*]

JOE [*to himself*]: Tha goes chunterin' i' th' pantry when somebody's at th' door. [*Rises, goes to door.*]

MRS PURDY'S VOICE: Is your mother in?

JOE: Yi, 'er's in right enough.

MRS PURDY: Well, then, can I speak to her?

JOE: [*calling*]: Mrs Purdy wants ter speak to thee, Mother.
[MRS GASCOIGNE *crosses the kitchen heavily, with a dripping-pan; stands in doorway.*]

MRS GASCOIGNE: Good afternoon.

MRS PURDY: Good afternoon.

MRS GASCOIGNE: Er – what is it?
[MRS PURDY *enters. She is a little fat, red-faced body in bonnet and black cape.*]

MRS PURDY: I wanted to speak to yer rather pertickler.

MRS GASCOIGNE [*giving way*]: Oh, yes?
[ALL THREE *enter the kitchen.* MRS PURDY *stands near the door.*]

MRS PURDY [*nodding at* JOE]: Has he had a haccident?

MRS GASCOIGNE: Broke his arm.

MRS PURDY: Oh my! that's nasty. When did 'e do that?

MRS GASCOIGNE: A wik sin' to-day.

MRS PURDY: In th' pit?

MRS GASCOIGNE: Yes – an's not goin' to get any accident pay – says as 'e worn't workin'; he wor foolin' about.

MRS PURDY: T-t-t-t! Did iver you know! I tell you what, missis, it's a wonder they let us live on the face o' the earth at all – it's a wonder we don't have to fly up i' th' air like birds.

JOE: There'd be a squark i' th' sky then!

MRS PURDY: But it is indeed. It's somethink awful. They've gave my mester a dirty job o' nights, at a guinea a week, an' he's worked fifty years for th' company, an' isn't but sixty-two now – said he wasn't equal to stall-workin', whereas he has to slave on th' roads an' comes whoam that tired he can't put's food in's mouth.

JOE: He's about like me.

MRS PURDY: Yis. But it's no nice thing, a guinea a week.

MRS GASCOIGNE: Well, that's how they're servin' 'em a' round – widders' coals stopped – leadin' raised to four-an'-eight – an' ivry man niggled down to nothink.

MRS PURDY: I wish I'd got that Fraser strung up by th' heels – I'd ma'e *his* sides o' bacon rowdy.

MRS GASCOIGNE: He's put a new manager to ivry pit, an' ivry one a nigger-driver.

MRS PURDY: Says he's got to economise – says the company's not a philanthropic concern –

MRS GASCOIGNE: But ta'es twelve hundred a year for hissen.

MRS PURDY: A mangy bachelor wi' 'is iron-men.

JOE: But they wunna work.

MRS PURDY: They say how he did but coss an' swear about them American Cutters. I should like to see one set outer 'im – they'd work hard enough rippin's guts out – even iron's got enough sense for that. [*She suddenly subsides.*]

    [*There is a pause.*]

MRS GASCOIGNE: How do you like living down Nether-green?

MRS PURDY: Well – we're very comfortable. It's small, but it's handy, an' sin' the mester's gone down t'a guinea –

MRS GASCOIGNE: It'll do for you three.

MRS PURDY: Yes.

    [*Another pause.*]

MRS GASCOIGNE: The men are comin' out again, they say.

MRS PURDY: Isn't it summat sickenin'? Well, I've werritted an' werritted till I'm soul-sick –

JOE: It sends yer that thin an' threadbare, y'have ter stop some-time.

MRS PURDY: There can be as much ache in a motherly body as in bones an' gristle, I'm sure o' that.

JOE: Nay, I'm more than bones an' gristle.

MRS PURDY: That's true as the day.

    [*Another long pause.*]

MRS GASCOIGNE: An' how have yer all bin keepin'?

MRS PURDY: Oh, very nicely – except our Bertha.

MRS GASCOIGNE: Is she poorly, then?

MRS PURDY: That's what I com ter tell yer. I niver knowed a word on't till a Sat'day, nor niver noticed a thing. Then she says to me, as white as a sheet, 'I've been sick every morning, Mother,' an' it com across me like a shot from a gun. I sunk down i' that chair an' couldna fetch a breath. – An' me as prided myself! I've often laughed about it, an' said I was thankful my children had all turned out so well, lads an' wenches as well, an' said it was a'cause they was all got of a Sunday – their father was too drunk a' Saturday, an' too tired o' wik-days. An' it's a fact, they've all turned out well, for I'd allers bin to chappil. Well, I've said it for a joke, but now it's turned on me. I'd better ha' kep' my tongue still.

JOE: It's not me, though, missis. I wish it wor.

MRS PURDY: There's no occasions to ma'e gam' of it neither, as far as I can see. The youngest an' the last of 'em as I've got, an' a lass as I liked, for she's simple, but she's good-natured, an' him a married man. Thinks I to myself, 'I'd better go to's mother, she'll ha'e more about 'er than's new wife – for she's a stuck-up piece o' goods as ever trod.'

MRS GASCOIGNE: Why, what d'yer mean?

MRS PURDY: I mean what I say – an' there's no denyin' it. That girl – well, it's nigh on breakin' my heart, for I'm that short o' breath. [Sighs.] I'm sure!

MRS GASCOIGNE: Why don't yer say what yer mean?

MRS PURDY: I've said it, haven't I? There's my gal gone four month wi' childt to your Luther.

MRS GASCOIGNE: Nay, nay, nay, missis! You'll never ma'e me believe it.

MRS PURDY: Glad would I be if I nedna. But I've gone through it all since Sat'day on. I've wanted to break every bone in 'er body – an' I've said I should on'y be happy if I was scraightin' at 'er funeral – an' I've said I'd wring his neck for 'im. But it doesn't alter it – there it is – an' there it will be. An' I s'll be a grandmother where my heart heaves, an' maun drag a wastrel baby through my old age. An' it's neither a cryin' nor a laughin' matter, but it's a matter of a girl wi' child, an' a man six week married.

MRS GASCOIGNE: But our Luther never went wi' your Bertha. How d'you make it out?

MRS PURDY: Yea, yea, missis – yea indeed.

JOE: Yi, Mother, he's bin out wi' 'er. She wor pals wi' Liza Ann Varley, as went out wi' Jim Horrocks. So Jim he passed Bertha onter our Luther. Why, I've had many a glass wi' the four of 'em, i' 'Th' Ram'.

MRS GASCOIGNE: I niver knowed nowt o' *this* afore.

JOE: Tha doesna know ivrythink, Mother.

MRS GASCOIGNE: An' it's well I don't, methinks.

JOE: Tha doesna want, neither.

MRS GASCOIGNE: Well, I dunno what we're goin' to do, missis. He's a young married man.

MRS PURDY: An' she's a girl o' mine.

MRS GASCOIGNE: How old is she?

MRS PURDY: She wor twenty-three last September.

MRS GASCOIGNE: Well then, I sh'd 'a thought she'd ha' known better.

MRS PURDY: An' what about him, missis, as goes and gets married t'r another fine madam d'rectly after he's been wi' my long lass?

JOE: But he never knowed owt about.

MRS PURDY: He'd seen th' blossom i' flower, if he hadna spotted the fruit a-comin'.

JOE: Yi – but –

MRS GASCOIGNE: Yi but what?

JOE: Well – you dunna expect – ivry time yer cast yer bread on th' wathers, as it'll come whoam to you like.

MRS GASCOIGNE: Well, I dunno what we're goin' to do.

MRS PURDY: I thought I'd better come to you, rather than –

JOE: Ah, you non want it gettin' about – an' *she'd* best not know – if it can be helped.

MRS GASCOIGNE: I can't see for why.

MRS PURDY: No indeed – a man as plays fast an' loose first wi' one an' then goes an' marries another stuck-up piece . . .

MRS GASCOIGNE: An' a wench as goes sittin' i' 'Th' Ram' wi' th' fellers mun expect what she gets, missis.

MRS PURDY: 'Appen so, 'appen so. An' th' man maun abide by what he's gi'en.

MRS GASCOIGNE: I dunno *what* we're goin' to do!

JOE: We'd best keep it as quiet as we can.

MRS PURDY: I thinks to mysen, 'It'll non become *me* to go an' jack up a married couple, for if *he's* at fault, it's her as 'ud ha'e ter suffer.' An' though she's haughty, I knowed her mother, as nice a body as ever stept, an' treated scandylos by Jim Hetherington. An', thinks I, she's a horphan, if she's got money, an' nobbut her husband i' th' world. Thinks I to mysen it's no good visitin' it on *'er* head, if he's a villain. For whatever th' men does, th' women maun ma'e up for. An' though I do consider as it's nowt b'r a dirty trick o' his'n to ta'e a poor lass like my long thing, an' go an' marry a woman wi' money –

MRS GASCOIGNE: Woman wi' money, an' peace go wi' 'er, 'er an' 'er money! What she's got, she'll keep, you take my word for it, missis.

MRS PURDY: Yes, an' she's right of it.

JOE: Nay, Mother, she's non close.

MRS GASCOIGNE: Isn't she? – oh, isn't she? An' what is she then? All she wanted was as much for her money as she could get. An' when she fun as nob'dy was for sale but our Luther, she says, 'Well, I'll take it.'

JOE: Nay, it worna like that – it wor him as wor that come-day-go-day –

MRS PURDY: God send Sunday.

MRS GASCOIGNE: An' what more canna man do, think yer, but ax a woman? When has *thee* ever done as much?

JOE: No, I hanna, 'cos I've niver seen th' woman as I wanted to say 'snap' – but he slormed an' she –

MRS GASCOIGNE: Slormed! Thee slorm but one fiftieth part to any lass thee likes, an' see if 'er's not all over thee afore tha's said six words. Slormed! 'Er wor that high an' mighty, 'er wanted summat bett'nor 'im.

JOE: Nay – I reckon he niver showed the spunk of a sprat-herring to 'er.

MRS GASCOIGNE: Did *thee* show any more? Hast iver done? Yet onybody 'ud think tha wor for marryin' 'er thysen.

JOE: If I'd ha' *bin* for marryin' 'er, I'd ha' gone wholesale, not ha' fudged and haffled.

MRS GASCOIGNE: But tha *worna* for marryin' neither 'er nor nobody.

JOE: No, I worna.

MRS GASCOIGNE: No, tha worna.

[*There is a long pause. The mother turns half apologetically, half explanatorily, to* MRS PURDY.]

It's like this 'ere, missis, if you'll not say nothink about it – sin' it's got to come out atween us. He courted Minnie Hetherington when she wor at her uncle's, at th' 'Bell o' Brass', an' he wor nowt bu'r a lad o' twenty-two, an' she twenty-one. An' he wor gone on 'er right enow. Then she had that row wi' 'er uncle, for she wor iver overbearin' an' chancy. Then our Luther says to me, 'I s'll ax 'er to marry me, Mother,' an' I says: 'Tha pleases thysen, but ter my thinkin' tha'rt a sight too young an' doesna know thy own mind.' Howsoever, much notice 'e takes o' me.

JOE: He took a lot o' notice on thee, tha knows well enough.

MRS GASCOIGNE: An' for what shouldn't he? Hadn't I bin a good mother to 'im i' ivry shape an' form? Let *her* make him as good a wife as I made him a mother! Well – we'll see. You'll see *him* repent the day. But they're not to be bidden. An' so, missis, he did ax 'er, as 'e'd said 'e should. But hoity-toity an' no thank yer, she wasna for havin' him, but mun go an' be a nursery governess up i' Manchester. Thinks I to myself, she's after a town johnny, a Bertie-Willie an' a yard o' cuffs. But he kep' on writin' to 'er, now an' again – an' she answered – as if she wor standin' at top of a flight of steps –

JOE: An' 'appen on'y wanted fetchin' down.

MRS GASCOIGNE: Wi' a kick from behint, if I'd ha' had th' doin' o't. So they go mornin' on. He sees 'er once i' a blew moon. If he goes ter Manchester, she condescends to see him for a couple of hours. If she comes here, she ca's i' this house wi' a 'how-do-you-do, Mrs Gascoigne', an' off again. If they go f'r a walk . . .

JOE: He's whoam again at nine o'clock.

MRS GASCOIGNE: If they go for a walk it's 'Thank you, I mustn't be very late. Good night, Luther.' I thought it ud niver come ter nothink. Then 'er uncle dies an' leaves her a hundred pounds, which considerin' th' way she'd been with 'im, was more than *I*'d ha' gen her – an' she was a bit nicer. She writes ter Luther ter come an' see 'er an' stop a couple o' days. He ta'es her to the the-etter, an's for goin' i' th' pit at a shillin', when she says: 'It's my treat, Luther, and five shillin' seats apiece, if you please.'

JOE: An' he couldna luik at th' performance, for fear as the folks was luikin' at 'im.

MRS GASCOIGNE: An' after th' the-etter, it must be supper wi' a man i' a tail-coat an' silver forks, an' she pays. 'Yes,' says I when he told me, 'that's the tricks of servants, showin' off afore decent folk.'

JOE: She could do what she liked, couldn't she?

MRS GASCOIGNE: Well, an' after that, he didna write, 'cept to say thank yer. For it put 'im in a horkard position. That wor four years ago, an' she's nobbut seen him three times sin' that. If she could but ha' snapped up somebody else, it 'ud bin good-bye to Luther –

JOE: As tha told him many a time.

MRS GASCOIGNE: As I told him many a time, for am I to sit an' see my own lad bitted an' bobbed, tasted an' spit out by a madam i' service? Then all of a suddin, three months back, come a letter: 'Dear Luther, I have been thinking it over, an' have come to the opinion that we'd better get married now, if we are ever goin' to. We've been dallying on all these years, and we seem to get no further. So we'd better make the plunge, if ever we're going to. Of course you will say exactly what you think. Don't agree to anything unless you want to. I only want to say that I think, if we're ever going to be married, we'd better do it without waiting any longer.' Well, missis, he got that letter when he com whoam fra work. I seed him porin' an' porin', but I says nowt. Then he ate some o's dinner, and went out. When he com in, it wor about haef past ten, an' 'e wor white as a sheet. He gen me that letter, an' says: 'What's think o' that, Mother?' Well, you could ha' knocked me down wi' a feather when I'd read it. I says: 'I think it's tidy cheek, my lad.' He took it back an' puts 's pocket, an' after a bit, 'e says: 'What should ter say, Mother?' 'Tha says what's a mind, my lad,' I says. So he begins unlacin' 's boots. Sudden he stops, an' wi's boot-tags rattlin', goes rummagin' for th' pen an' ink. 'What art goin' to say?' I says. 'I'm goin' ter say, 'er can do as 'er's a mind. If 'er wants ter be married, 'er can, an' if 'er doesna, 'er nedna.' So I thinks we could leave it at that. He sits him down, an' doesna write more nor a side an' a haef. I thinks: 'That's done it, it'll be an end between them two now.' He niver gen th' letter to me to read.

JOE: He did to me. He says: 'I'm ready an' willin' to do what you want, whenever yer want. I'm earnin' about thirty-five bob a week, an' haven't got any money because my mother gi'es me what I ax for ter spend. But I can have what I ask for to set up house with. Your loving – Luther.' He says to me: 'Dost think it's a'right?' I says: 'I s'd think so; 'er maun ma'e what 'er likes out on't.'

MRS GASCOIGNE: On th' Monday after, she wor here livin' at 'er A'nt's an' th' notice was in at th' registrar. I says: 'What money dost want?' He says: 'Thee buy what tha thinks we s'll want.' So he tells Minnie, an' she says: 'Not bi-out I'm theer.' Well, we goes ter Nottingham, an' she will ha'e nowt b'r old-fashioned stuff. I says: 'That's niver *my* mind, Minnie.' She says: 'Well, I like it, an' yo'll see it'll look nice. I'll pay for it.' Which to be sure I never let her. For she'd had a mester as made a fool of her, tellin' her this an' that, what wor good taste, what wor bad.

JOE: An' it *does* look nice, Mother, their house.

MRS GASCOIGNE: We'll see how it looks i' ten years' time, my lad, wi' th' racket an' tacket o' children. For it's not serviceable, missis.

MRS PURDY [*who has been a sympathetic and exclamative listener*]: Then it's no good.

MRS GASCOIGNE: An' that's how they got married.

JOE: An' he went about wi's tail atween his legs, scared outer's life.

MRS GASCOIGNE: For I said no more. If he axed me owt, I did it; if he wanted owt, I got it. But it wasn't for me to go interferin' where I wasn't wanted.

JOE: If ever I get married, Mother, I s'll go i' lodgin's six month aforehand.

MRS GASCOIGNE: Tha'd better – ter get thysen a bit case-hardened.

JOE: Yi. But I'm goin' t'r Australia.

MRS GASCOIGNE: I come withee, then.

JOE: Tha doesna.

MRS GASCOIGNE: I dunna fret – tha'lt non go.

MRS PURDY: Well, it was what I should call a bit off-hand, I must say.

MRS GASCOIGNE: You can see now how he got married, an' who's to blame.

JOE: Nay, yo' canna ma'e 'er to blame for Bertha. Liza Ann Varley's ter blame for th' lass goin' out o' nights.

MRS PURDY: An' there I thought they wor both i' Varley's – not gallivantin'.

JOE: They often was. An' Jim Horrocks is ter blame fer couplin' 'er onter our Luther, an' him an' her's ter blame for the rest. I dunno how you can lay it on Minnie. You might as well lay it on 'er if th' childt wor mine.

MRS GASCOIGNE [*sharply*]: Tha'd ha'e more sense!

JOE: I'd try.

MRS GASCOIGNE: But now she's played fast an' loose wi' him – twice I *know* he axed 'er to ha'e him – now she's asked for what she's got. She's put her puddin' in her mouth, an' if she's burnt herself, serve her right.

MRS PURDY: Well, I didn't want to go to court. I thought, his mother'll be th' best one to go to –

MRS GASCOIGNE: No – you mun go to him hisself – go an'

tell him i' front of her – an' if she wants anythink, she mun ma'e arrangements herself.

JOE: What was you thinkin' of, Missis Purdy?

MRS PURDY: Well, I was thinkin', she's a poor lass – an' I didn't want 'er to go to court, for they ax such questions – an' I thought it was such a *thing*, him six wik married – though to be sure I'd no notions of how it was – I thought, we might happen say, it was one o' them electricians as was along when they laid th' wires under th' road down to Batsford – and –

JOE: And arrange for a lump sum, like?

MRS PURDY: Yes – we're poor, an' she's poor – an' if she had a bit o' money of 'er own – for we should niver touch it – it might be a inducement to some other young feller – for, poor long thing, she's that simple –

MRS GASCOIGNE: Well, ter my knowledge, them as has had a childt seems to get off i' marriage better nor many as hasn't. I'm sure, there's a lot o' men likes it, if they think a woman's had a baby by another man.

MRS PURDY: That's nothing to trust by, missis; you'll say so yourself.

JOE: An' about how much do you want? Thirty pounds?

MRS PURDY: We want what's fair. I got it fra Emma Stapleton; they had forty wi' their Lucy.

JOE: Forty pound?

MRS PURDY: Yes.

MRS GASCOIGNE: Well, then, let *her* find it. She's paid for nothing but the wedding. She's got money enough, if he's none. Let *her* find it. She made the bargain, she maun stick by it. It was her dip i' th' bran-tub – if there's a mouse nips hold of her finger, she maun suck it better, for nobody axed her to dip.

MRS PURDY: You think I'd better go to him? Eh, missis, it's a nasty business. But right's right.

MRS GASCOIGNE: Right *is* right, Mrs Purdy. And you go tell him a-front of her – that's the best thing you can do. Then iverything's straight.

MRS PURDY: But for her he might ha' married our Bertha.

MRS GASCOIGNE: To be sure, to be sure.

MRS PURDY: What right had she to snatch when it pleased her?

MRS GASCOIGNE: That's what I say. If th' woman ca's for th' piper, th' woman maun pay th' tune.

MRS PURDY: Not but what –

JOE: It's a nasty business.

MRS GASCOIGNE: Nasty or not, it's hers now, not mine. He's *her* husband. 'My son's my son till he takes him a wife,' an' no longer. Now let her answer for it.

MRS PURDY: An' you think I'd better go when they're both in?

MRS GASCOIGNE: I should go to-night, atween six an' seven, that's what I should do.

JOE: I never should. If I was you, I'd settle it wi'out Minnie's knowin' – it's bad enough.

MRS GASCOIGNE: What's bad enough?

JOE: Why, that.

MRS GASCOIGNE: What?

JOE: Him an' 'er – it's bad enough as it is.

MRS GASCOIGNE [*with great bitterness*]: Then let it be a bit worse, let it be a bit worse. Let her have it, then; it'll do her good. Who is she, to trample eggs that another hen would sit warm? No – Mrs Purdy, *give* it her. It'll take her down a peg or two, and, my sirs, she wants it, my sirs, she needs it!

JOE [*muttering*]: A fat lot o' good it'll do.

MRS GASCOIGNE: What has thee ter say, I should like to know? Fed an' clothed an' coddled, tha art, an' not a thing tha lacks. But wait till I'm gone, my lad; tha'lt know what I've done for thee, then, tha will.

JOE: For a' that, it's no good 'er knowin'.

MRS GASCOIGNE: Isna it? – isna it? If it's not good for 'er, it's good for '*im*.

JOE: I dunna believe it.

MRS GASCOIGNE: Who asked *thee* to believe it? Tha's showed thysen a wise man *this* day, hasn't ter? Wheer should ter be terday but for me? Wheer should ter iver ha' bin? An' then *tha* sits up for to talk. It ud look better o' thee not to spit i' th' hand as holds thy bread an' butter.

JOE: Neither do I.

MRS GASCOIGNE: Doesn't ter! Tha has a bit too much chelp an' chunter. It doesna go well, my lad. Tha wor blortin' an' bletherin' down at th' office a bit sin', an' a mighty fool tha made o' thysen. How should thee like to go home wi' *thy* tale o' to-day, to Minnie, might I ax thee?

JOE: If she didna like it, she could lump it.

MRS GASCOIGNE: It 'ud be thee as 'ud lump, my lad. But what does thee know about it? 'Er's rip th' guts out on thee like a tiger, an' stan' grinnin' at thee when tha shrivelled up 'cause tha'd no inside left.

MRS PURDY: She looks it, I must admit – every bit of it.

JOE: For a' that, it's no good her knowing.

MRS GASCOIGNE: Well, I say it *is* – an' thee, tha shiftly little know-all, as blorts at one minute like a suckin' calf an' th' next blethers like a hass, dunna thee come layin' th' law down to me, for I know better. No, Mrs Purdy, it's no good comin' to me. You've a right to some compensation, an' that lass o' yours has; but let them as cooked the goose eat it, that's all. Let him arrange it hisself – an' if he does nothink, put him i' court, that's all.

MRS PURDY: He's not goin' scot-free, you may back your life o' that.

MRS GASCOIGNE: You go down to-night atween six an' seven, an' let 'em have it straight. You know where they live?

MRS PURDY: I' Simson Street?

MRS GASCOIGNE: About four houses up – next Holbrooks.

MRS PURDY [*rising*]: Yes.

JOE: An' it'll do no good. Gi'e me th' money, Mother; I'll pay it.

MRS GASCOIGNE: Tha wunna!

JOE: I've a right to th' money – I've addled it.

MRS GASCOIGNE: A' right – an' I've saved it for thee. But tha has none on't till tha knocks me down an' ta'es it out o' my pocket.

MRS PURDY: No – let them pay themselves. It's not thy childt, is it?

JOE: It isna — but the money is.

MRS GASCOIGNE: We'll see.

MRS PURDY: Well, I mun get back. Thank yer, missis.

MRS GASCOIGNE: And thank *you*! I'll come down to-morrow — at dark hour.

MRS PURDY: Thank yer. — I hope yer arm'll soon be better.

JOE: Thank yer.

MRS GASCOIGNE: I'll come down to-morrow. You'll go to-night — atween six an' seven?

MRS PURDY: Yes — if it mun be done, it mun. He took his own way, she took hers, now I mun take mine. Well, good afternoon. I mun see about th' mester's dinner.

JOE: And you haven't said nothink to nobody?

MRS PURDY: I haven't — I shouldn't be flig, should I?

JOE: No — I should keep it quiet as long's you can.

MRS GASCOIGNE: There's no need for a' th' world to know — but them as is concerned maun abide by it.

MRS PURDY: Well, good afternoon.

MRS GASCOIGNE: Good afternoon.

JOE: Good afternoon.

[*Exit* MRS PURDY.]

Well, that's a winder!

MRS GASCOIGNE: Serve her right, for tip-callin' wi'm all those years.

JOE: She niver ought to know.

MRS GASCOIGNE: I — I could fetch thee a wipe ower th' face, I could!

[*He sulks. She is in a rage.*]

SCENE II

The kitchen of LUTHER GASCOIGNE'S *new home. It is pretty — in 'cottage' style; rush-bottomed chairs, black oak-bureau, brass candlesticks, delft, etc. Green cushions in chairs. Towards five o'clock. Firelight. It is growing dark.*

MINNIE GASCOIGNE *is busy about the fire: a tall, good-looking young woman, in a shirt-blouse and dark skirt, and apron. She lifts*

*lids of saucepans, etc., hovers impatiently, looks at clock, begins to
trim lamp.*

MINNIE: I wish he'd come. If I didn't want him, he'd be here
half-an-hour since. But just because I've got a pudding that
wants eating on the tick ... ! He – he's *never* up to the
cratch; he never is. As if the day wasn't long enough!
[*Sound of footsteps. She seizes a saucepan, and is rushing towards the door. The latch has clacked.* LUTHER *appears in the
doorway, in his pit-dirt – a collier of medium height, with fair
moustache. He has a red scarf knotted round his throat, and a
cap with a Union medal. The two almost collide.*]

LUTHER: My word, you're on the hop!

MINNIE [*disappearing into scullery*]: You *nearly* made me drop
the saucepan. Why are you so late?

LUTHER: I'm non late, am I?

MINNIE: You're twenty minutes later than yesterday.

LUTHER: Oh ah, I stopped finishing a stint, an' com up wi'
a'most th' last batch. [*He takes a tin bottle and a dirty calico
snap-bag out of his pocket, puts them on the bureau; goes into the
scullery.*]

MINNIE'S VOICE: No! [*She comes hurrying out with the saucepan.
In a moment,* LUTHER *follows. He has taken off his coat and cap,
his heavy trousers are belted round his hips, his arms are bare to
above the elbow, because the pit-singlet of thick flannel is almost
sleeveless.*]

LUTHER: Tha *art* throng!

MINNIE [*at the fire, flushed*]: Yes, and everything's ready, and
will be spoiled.

LUTHER: Then we'd better eat it afore I wash me.

MINNIE: No – no – it's not nice –

LUTHER: Just as ter's a mind – but there's scarce a collier in a
thousand washes hissen afore he has his dinner. We never
did a-whoam.

MINNIE: But it doesn't look nice.

LUTHER: Eh, wench, tha'lt soon get used ter th' looks on me.
A bit o' dirt's like a veil on my face – I shine through th'
'andsomer. What hast got? [*He peers over her range.*]

MINNIE [*waving a fork*]: You're not to look.

LUTHER: It smells good.

MINNIE: Are you *going* to have your dinner like that?

LUTHER: Ay, lass – just for once. [*He spreads a newspaper in one of the green-cushioned armchairs and sits down. She disappears into the scullery with a saucepan. He takes off his great pit-boots. She sets a soup-tureen on the table, and lights the lamp. He watches her face in the glow.*] Tha'rt non bad-luikin' when ter's a mind.

MINNIE: *When* have I a mind?

LUTHER: Tha's allers a mind – but when ter lights th' lamp tha'rt i' luck's way.

MINNIE: Come on, then.

    [*He drags his chair to the table.*]

LUTHER: I s'll ha'e ter ha'e a newspaper afront on me, or thy cloth'll be a blackymoor. [*Begins disarranging the pots.*]

MINNIE: Oh, you *are* a nuisance! [*Jumps up.*]

LUTHER: I can put 'em a' back again.

MINNIE: I know your puttings back.

LUTHER: Tha couldna get married by thysen, could ter? – so tha'lt ha'e ter ma'e th' best on me.

MINNIE: But you're such a bother – never here at the right time – never doing the right thing –

LUTHER: An' my mouth's ter wide an' my head's ter narrow. Shalt iver ha' come ter th' end of my faults an' failin's?

MINNIE [*giving him soup*]: I wish I could.

LUTHER: An' now tha'lt snap mu head off 'cos I slobber, shanna tha?

MINNIE: Then don't slobber.

LUTHER: I'll try my luck. What hast bin doin' a'day?

MINNIE: Working.

LUTHER: Has our Joe bin in?

MINNIE: No. I rather thought he might, but he hasn't.

LUTHER: You've not been up home?

MINNIE: To your mother's? No, what should I go there for?

LUTHER: Eh, I dunno what ter should go for – I thought tha 'appen might.

MINNIE: But what for?

LUTHER: Nay – I niver thowt nowt about what for.

MINNIE: Then why did you ask me?

LUTHER: I dunno.

[*A pause.*]

MINNIE: Your mother can come here, can't she?

LUTHER: Ay, she can come. Tha'll be goin' up wi' me to-night – I want ter go an' see about our Joe.

MINNIE: What about him?

LUTHER: How he went on about's club money. Shall ter come wi' me?

MINNIE: I wanted to do my curtains.

LUTHER: But tha's got a' day to do them in.

MINNIE: But I want to do them to-night – I feel like it.

LUTHER: A' right. – I shanna be long, at any rate.

[*A pause.*]

What dost keep lookin' at?

MINNIE: How?

LUTHER: Tha keeps thy eye on me rarely.

MINNIE [*laughing*]: It's your mouth – it looks so red and bright, in your black face.

LUTHER: Does it look nasty to thee?

MINNIE: No – no-o.

LUTHER [*pushing his moustache, laughing*]: It ma'es you look like a nigger, i' your pit-dirt – th' whites o' your eyes!

MINNIE: Just. [*She gets up to take his plate; goes and stands beside him. He lifts his face to her.*] I want to see if I can see you; you look so different.

LUTHER: Tha can see me well enough. Why dost want to?

MINNIE: It's almost like having a stranger.

LUTHER: Would ter rather?

MINNIE: What?

LUTHER: Ha'e a stranger?

MINNIE: What for?

LUTHER: Hao – I dunno.

MINNIE [*touching his hair*]: You look rather nice – an' your hair's so dirty.

LUTHER: Gi'e me a kiss.

MINNIE: But where? You're all grime.

LUTHER: I'm sure I've licked my mouth clean.

MINNIE [*stooping suddenly, and kissing him*]: You don't look nearly such a tame rabbit, in your pit-dirt.

LUTHER [*catching her in his arms*]: Dunna I? [*Kisses her.*] What colour is my eyes?

MINNIE: Bluey-grey.

LUTHER: An' thine's grey an' black.

MINNIE: Mind! [*She looks at her blouse when he releases her.*]

LUTHER [*timid*]: Have I blacked it?

MINNIE: A bit. [*She goes to the scullery; returns with another dish.*]

LUTHER: They talkin' about comin' out again.

MINNIE [*returning*]: Good laws! – they've no need.

LUTHER: They are, though.

MINNIE: It's a holiday they want.

LUTHER: Nay, it isna. They want th' proper scale here, just as they ha'e it ivrywhere else.

MINNIE: But if the seams are thin, and the company can't afford . . .

LUTHER: They can afford a' this gret new electric plant; they can afford to build new houses for managers, an' ter give blo – ter give Frazer twelve hundred a year.

MINNIE: If they want a good manager to make the pits pay, they have to give him a good salary.

LUTHER: So's he can clip down our wages.

MINNIE: Why, what are yours clipped down?

LUTHER: Mine isn't, but there's plenty as is.

MINNIE: And will this strike make a butty of you?

LUTHER: You don't strike to get made a butty on.

MINNIE: Then how *do* you do it? You're thirty-one.

LUTHER: An' there's many as owd as me as is day-men yet.

MINNIE: But there's more that aren't, that are butties.

LUTHER: Ay, they've had luck.

MINNIE: Luck! You mean they've had some *go* in them.

LUTHER: Why, what can I do more than I am doin'?

MINNIE: It isn't what you do, it's how you do it. Sluther through any job; get to th' end of it, no matter how. That's you.

LUTHER: I hole a stint as well as any man.

MINNIE: Then I back it takes you twice as long.

LUTHER: Nay, nor that neither.

MINNIE: I *know* you're not much of a workman – I've heard it from other butties, that you never put your heart into anything.

LUTHER: Who hast heard it fra?

MINNIE: From those that know. And I could ha' told it *them*, for I know you. You'll be a day-man at seven shillings a day till the end of your life – and you'll be satisfied, so long as you can shilly-shally through. That's what your mother did for you – mardin' you up till you were all mard-soft.

LUTHER: Tha's got a lot ter say a' of a suddin. Thee shut thy mouth.

MINNIE: You've been dragged round at your mother's apron-strings, all the lot of you, till there isn't half a man among you.

LUTHER: Tha seems fond enough of our Joe.

MINNIE: He is th' best in the bunch.

LUTHER: Tha should ha' married him, then.

MINNIE: I shouldn't have had to ask *him*, if he was ready.

LUTHER: I'd axed thee twice afore – tha knowed tha could ha'e it when ter wanted.

MINNIE: *Axed* me! It was like asking me to pull out a tooth for you.

LUTHER: Yi, an' it felt like it.

MINNIE: What?

LUTHER: Axin' thee to marry me. I'm blessed if it didna feel like axin' the doctor to pull ten teeth out of a stroke.

MINNIE: And then you expect me to have you!

LUTHER: Well, tha *has* done, whether or not.

MINNIE: I – yes, I had to fetch you, like a mother fetches a kid from school. A pretty sight you looked. Didn't your mother give you a ha'penny to spend, to get you to go?

LUTHER: No; she spent it for me.

MINNIE: She would! She wouldn't even let you spend your own ha'penny. You'd have lost it, or let somebody take it from you.

LUTHER: Yi. Thee.

MINNIE: Me! – me take anything from you! Why, you've got nothing worth having.

LUTHER: I dunno – tha seems ter think so sometimes.

MINNIE: Oh! Shilly-shally and crawl, that's all you can do. You ought to have stopped with your mother.

LUTHER: I should ha' done, if tha hadna hawksed me out.

MINNIE: You aren't *fit* for a woman to have married, you're not.

LUTHER: Then why did thee marry me? It wor thy doin's.

MINNIE: Because I could get nobody better.

LUTHER: I'm more class than I thought for, then.

MINNIE: Are you! Are you!

[JOE'S *voice is heard.*]

JOE: I'm comin' in, you two, so stop snaggin' an' snarlin'.

LUTHER: Come in; 'er'll 'appen turn 'er tap on thee.

[JOE *enters.*]

JOE: Are you eatin' yet?

LUTHER: Ay – it ta'es 'er that long ter tell my sins. Tha's just come right for puddin'. Get thee a plate outer t'cupboard – an' a spoon outer t'basket.

JOE [*at the cupboard*]: You've got ivrythink tip-top. What should ter do if I broke thee a plate, Minnie?

MINNIE: I should break another over your head.

[*He deliberately drops and smashes a plate. She flushes crimson.*]

LUTHER: Well, I'm glad it worna me.

JOE: I'm that clumsy wi' my left 'and, Minnie! Why doesna ter break another ower my head?

LUTHER [*rising and putting pudding on a plate*]: Here, ta'e this an' sit thee down.

[*His brother seats himself.*]

Hold thy knees straight, an' for God's sake dunna thee break this. Can ter manage?

JOE: I reckon so. If I canna, Minnie'll feed me wi' a spoon. Shonna ter?

MINNIE: Why did you break my plate?

JOE: Nay, I didna break it – it wor the floor.

MINNIE: You did it on purpose.

JOE: How could I? I didn't say ter th' floor: 'Break thou this plate, O floor!'

MINNIE: You have no right.

JOE [*addressing the floor*]: Tha'd no right to break that plate –
dost hear? I'd a good mind ter drop a bit o' puddin' on thy
face. [*He balances the spoon; the plate slides down from his knee,
smash into the fender.*]

MINNIE [*screams*]: It's my best service! [*Begins to sob.*]

LUTHER: Nay, our Joe!

JOE: 'Er's no occasions ter scraight. I bought th' service an' I
can get th' plates matched. What's her grizzlin' about?

MINNIE: I shan't ask you to get them matched.

JOE: Dunna thee, an' then tha runs no risk o' bein' denied.

MINNIE: What have you come here like this for?

JOE: I haena come here like this. I come ter tell yer our
Harriet says, would yer mind goin' an' tellin' 'er what she
can do with that childt's coat, as she's made a' wrong. If
you'd looked slippy, I'd ha' ta'en yer ter th' Cinematograph after. But, dearly-beloved brethren, let us weep;
these our dear departed dinner-plates ... Come, Minnie,
drop a tear as you pass by.

LUTHER [*to* MINNIE]: Tha needna fret, Minnie, they can easy
be matched again.

MINNIE: You're just pleased to see him make a fool of me,
aren't you?

LUTHER: He's non made a fool o' thee – tha's made a fool o'
thysen, scraightin' an' carryin' on.

JOE: It's a fact, Minnie. Nay, let me kiss thee better.
[*She has risen, with shut face.*
*He approaches with outstretched left arm. She swings round, fetches
him a blow over his upper right arm. He bites his lip with pain.*]

LUTHER [*rising*]: Has it hurt thee, lad? Tha shouldna fool wi'
her.
[MINNIE *watches the two brothers with tears of mortification
in her eyes. Then she throws off her apron, pins on her hat, puts
on her coat, and is marching out of the house.*]

LUTHER: Are you going to Harriet's?

JOE: I'll come and fetch you in time for th' Cinematograph.
[*The door is heard to bang.*]

JOE [*picking up broken fragments of plates*]: That's done it.

LUTHER: It's bad luck – ne'er mind. How art goin' on?

JOE: Oh, alright.

LUTHER: What about thy club money?

JOE: They wunna gi'e't me. But, I say, sorry – tha'rt for it.

LUTHER: Ay – I dunno what 'er married me for, f'r it's nowt bu' fault she finds wi' me, from th' minnit I come i' th' house to th' minnit I leave it.

JOE: Dost wish tha'd niver done it? – niver got married?

LUTHER [*sulky*]: I dunno – sometimes.

JOE [*with tragic emphasis*]: Then it's the blasted devil!

LUTHER: I dunno – I'm married to 'er, an' she's married to me, so she can pick holes i' me as much as she likes –

JOE: As a rule, she's nice enough wi' me.

LUTHER: She's nice wi' ivrybody but me.

JOE: An' dost ter care?

LUTHER: Ay – I do.

JOE: Why doesn't ter go out an' leave her?

LUTHER: I dunno.

JOE: By the Lord, she'd cop it if I had 'er.
     [*Pause.*]

LUTHER: I wor comin' up to-night.

JOE: I thought tha would be. But there's Mrs Purdy comin' ter see thee.

LUTHER: There's who?

JOE: Mrs Purdy. Didna ter ha'e a bit of a go wi' their Bertha, just afore Minnie wrote thee?

LUTHER: Ay. Why?

JOE: 'Er mother says she's wi' childt by thee. She come up ter my mother this afternoon, an' said she wor comin' here to-night.

LUTHER: Says what?

JOE: Says as their Bertha's goin' ter ha'e a child, an' 'er lays it on ter thee.

LUTHER: Oh, my good God!

JOE: Isna it right?

LUTHER: It's right if 'er says so.

JOE: Then it's the blasted devil! [*A pause.*] So I come on here ter see if I could get Minnie to go up to our Harriet.

LUTHER: Oh, my good God!

JOE: I thought, if we could keep it from 'er, we might settle summat, an' 'er niver know.

LUTHER [*slowly*]: My God alive!

JOE: She said she'd hush it up, an' lay it ont'r a electrician as laid th' cable, an' is gone goodness knows where – make an arrangement, for forty pound.

LUTHER [*thoughtfully*]: I wish I wor struck dead.

JOE: Well, tha arena', an' so tha'd better think about it. My mother said as Minnie ought to know, but I say diff'rent, an' if Mrs Purdy doesna tell her, nobody need.

LUTHER: I wish I wor struck dead. I wish a ton o' rock 'ud fa' on me to-morrer.

JOE: It wunna for wishin'.

LUTHER: My good God!

JOE: An' so – I'll get thee forty quid, an' lend it thee. When Mrs Purdy comes, tell her she shall ha'e twenty quid this day week, an' twenty quid a year from now, if thy name's niver been mentioned. I believe 'er's a clat-fart.

LUTHER: Me a childt by Bertha Purdy! But – but what's that for – now there's Minnie?

JOE: I dunno what it's for, but theer it is, as I'm tellin' thee. I'll stop for another ha'ef an hour, an' if 'er doesna come, tha mun see to 'er by thysen.

LUTHER: 'Er'll be back afore ha'ef an hour's up. Tha mun go an' stop 'er . . . I – I niver meant – Look here, our Joe, I – if I – if she – if she – My God, what have I done now!

JOE: We can stop her from knowin'.

LUTHER [*looking round*]: She'll be comin' back any minnit. Nay, I niver meant t'r ha'. Joe . . .

JOE: What?

LUTHER: She – she –

JOE: 'Er niver ned know.

LUTHER: Ah, but though . . .

JOE: What?

LUTHER: I – I – I've *done* it.

JOE: Well, it might ha' happened t'r anybody.

LUTHER: But when 'er knows – an' it's *me* as has done it . . .

JOE: It wouldn't ha' mattered o' anyhow, if it had bin sumb'dy else. But tha knows what ter's got ter say. Arena' ter goin' ter wesh thee? Go an' get th' panchion.

LUTHER [*rising*]: 'Er'll be comin' in any minnit.

JOE: Get thee weshed, man.

LUTHER [*fetching a bucket and lading-can from the scullery, and emptying water from the boiler*]: Go an' ta'e 'er somewhere, while Mrs Purdy goes, sholl ter?

JOE: D'rectly. Tha heered what I telled thee?
[*There is a noise of splashing in the scullery. Then a knock.* JOE *goes to the door. He is heard saying 'Come in.'
Enter* MRS PURDY.]

MRS PURDY: I hope I've not come a-mealtimes.

JOE: No, they've finished. Minnie's gone up t'r our Harriet's.

MRS PURDY: Thank the Lord for small mercies – for I didn't fancy sittin' an' tellin' her about our Bertha.

JOE: We dunna want 'er ter know. Sit thee down.

MRS PURDY: I'm of that mind, mester, I am. As I said, what's th' good o' jackin' up a young married couple? For it won't unmarry 'em nor ma'e things right. An' yet, my long lass oughtner ter bear a' th' brunt.

JOE: Well, an' 'er isna goin' to.

MRS PURDY: Is that Mester weshin'?

JOE: Ah.

MRS PURDY: 'As ter towd him?

JOE: Ah.

MRS PURDY: Well, it's none o' my wishin's, I'm sure o' that. Eh, dear, you've bin breakin' th' crockery a'ready!

JOE: Yes, that's me, bein' wallit.

MRS PURDY: T-t-t! So this is 'ow she fancied it?

JOE: Ah, an' it non luiks bad, does it?

MRS PURDY: Very natty. Very nice an' natty.

JOE [*taking up the lamp*]: Come an' look at th' parlour.
[JOE *and* MRS PURDY *exit R.*]

MRS PURDY'S VOICE: Yis – yis – it's nice an' plain. But a bit o' red plush is 'andsomer, to my mind. It's th' old-fashioned style, like! My word, but them three ornyments is gaudy-lookin'.

JOE: An' they reckon they're worth five pound. 'Er mester gen 'em 'er.

MRS PURDY: I'd rather had th' money.

JOE: Ah, me an' a'.

[*During this time,* LUTHER *has come hurrying out of the scullery into the kitchen, rubbing his face with a big roller-towel. He is naked to the waist. He kneels with his knees on the fender, sitting on his heels, rubbing himself. His back is not washed. He rubs his hair dry.*

Enter JOE, *with the lamp, followed by* MRS PURDY.]

MRS PURDY: It's uncommon, very uncommon, Mester Gaskin – and looks well, too, for them as likes it. But it hardly goes wi' my fancy, somehow, startin' wi' second-hand, owd-fashioned stuff. You dunno *who's* sotten themselves on these 'ere chairs, now, do you?

LUTHER: It ma'es no diff'rence to me who's sot on 'em an' who 'asna.

MRS PURDY: No – you get used to'm.

LUTHER [*to* JOE]: Shall thee go up t'r our Harriet's?

JOE: If ter's a mind. [*Takes up his cap. To* MRS PURDY] An' you two can settle as best you can.

MRS PURDY: Yes – yes. I'm not one for baulkin' mysen an' cuttin' off my nose ter spite my face.

[LUTHER *has finished wiping himself. He takes a shifting shirt from the bureau, and struggles into it; then goes into the scullery.*]

JOE: An' you sure you'll keep it quiet, missis?

MRS PURDY: Am I goin' bletherin' up street an' down street, think yer?

JOE: An' dunna tell your Bob.

MRS PURDY: I've more sense. There's not a word 'e 'ears a-whoam as is of any count, for out it 'ud leak when he wor canned. Yes, my guyney – we know what our mester is.

[*Re-enter* LUTHER, *in shirt and black trousers. He drops his pit-trousers and singlet beside the hearth.*

MRS PURDY *bends down and opens his pit-trousers.*]

MRS PURDY: Nay, if ter drops 'em of a heap, they niver goin' ter get dry an' cosy. Tha sweats o' th' hips, as my lads did.

LUTHER: Well, go thy ways, Joe.

JOE: Ay – well – good luck. An' good night, Mrs Purdy.

MRS PURDY: Good night.

[*Exit* JOE. *There are several moments of silence.* LUTHER *puts the broken pots on the table.*]

MRS PURDY: It's sad work, Mester Gaskin, f'r a' on us.

LUTHER: Ay.

MRS PURDY: I left that long lass o' mine fair gaunt, fair chalked of a line, I did, poor thing. Not bu' what 'er should 'a 'ad more sense.

LUTHER: Ah!

MRS PURDY: But it's no use throwin' good words after bad deeds. Not but what it's a nasty thing for yer t'r 'a done, it is – an' yer can scarce look your missis i' th' face again, I should think. [*Pause.*] But I says t'r our Bertha, 'It's his'n, an' he mun pay!' Eh, but how 'er did but scraight an' cry. It fair turned me ower. 'Dunna go to 'm, Mother,' 'er says, 'dunna go to 'm for to tell him!' 'Yi,' I says, 'right's right – tha doesna get off wi' nowt, nor shall 'e neither. 'E wor but a scamp to do such a thing,' I says, yes, I did. For you was older nor 'er. Not but what she was old enough ter ha'e more sense. But 'er wor allers one o' th' come-day-go-day sort, as 'ud gi'e th' clothes off 'er back an' niver know 'er wor nek'd – a gra't soft looney as she is, an' serves 'er right for bein' such a gaby. Yi, an' I believe 'er wor fond on thee – if a wench can be fond of a married man. For one blessing, 'er doesna know what 'er wor an' what 'er worn't. For they mau talk o' bein' i' love – but you non in love wi' onybody, wi'out they's a chance o' their marryin' you – howiver much you may like 'em. An' I'm thinkin', th' childt'll set 'er up again when it comes, for 'er's gone that wezzel-brained an' doited, I'm sure! An' it's a mort o' trouble for me, mester, a sight o' trouble it is. Not as I s'll be hard on 'er. She knowed I wor comin' 'ere to-night, an's not spoke a word for hours. I left 'er sittin' on th' sofey hangin' 'er 'ead. But it's a weary business, mester, an' nowt ter be proud on. I s'd think tha wishes tha'd niver clapt eyes on our Bertha.

LUTHER [*thinking hard*]: I dunna – I dunna. An' I dunna wish as I'd niver seen 'er, no, I dunna. 'Er liked me, an' I liked 'er.

MRS PURDY: An' 'appen, but for this 'ere marriage o' thine, tha'd 'a married 'er.

LUTHER: Ah, I should. F'r 'er liked me, an' 'er worna neither nice nor near, nor owt else, an' 'er'd bin fond o' me.

MRS PURDY: 'Er would, an' it's a thousand pities. But what's done's done.

LUTHER: Ah, I know that.

MRS PURDY: An' as for yer missis –

LUTHER: 'Er mun do as 'er likes.

MRS PURDY: But tha'rt not for tellin' 'er?

LUTHER: 'Er – 'er'll know some time or other.

MRS PURDY: Nay, nay, 'er nedna. You married now, lad, an' you canna please yoursen.

LUTHER: It's a fact.

MRS PURDY: An' Lizzy Stapleton, she had forty pound wi' 'er lad, an' it's not as if you hadn't got money. An' to be sure, we've none.

LUTHER: No, an' I've none.

MRS PURDY: Yes, you've some atween you – an' – well ...

LUTHER: I can get some.

MRS PURDY: Then what do you say?

LUTHER: I say as Bertha's welcome t'r any forty pounds, if I'd got it. For – for – missis, she wor better to me than iver my wife's bin.

MRS PURDY [*frightened by his rage*]: Niver, lad!

LUTHER: She wor – ah but though she wor. She thought a lot on me.

MRS PURDY: An' so I'm sure your missis does. She naggles thy heart out, maybe. But that's just the wrigglin' a place out for hersen. She'll settle down comfortable, lad.

LUTHER [*bitterly*]: Will she?

MRS PURDY: Yi – yi. An' tha's done 'er a crewel wrong, my lad. An' tha's done my gel one as well. For, though she was old enough to know better, yet she's good-hearted and trustin', an' 'ud gi'e 'er shoes off 'er feet. An' tha's landed 'er, tha knows. For it's not th' bad women as 'as bastards nowadays – they've a sight too much gumption. It's fools like our'n – poor thing.

LUTHER: I've done everything that was bad, I know that.

MRS PURDY: Nay – nay – young fellers, they are like that. But it's wrong, for look at my long lass sittin' theer on that sofey, as if 'er back wor broke.

LUTHER [*loudly*]: But I dunna wish I'd niver seen 'er, I dunna. It wor – it wor – she wor good to me, she wor, an' I dunna wish I'd niver done it.

MRS PURDY: Then tha ought, that's a'. For I do – an' 'er does.

LUTHER: Does 'er say 'er wishes 'er'd niver seen me?

MRS PURDY: 'Er says nowt o' nohow.

LUTHER: Then 'er doesna wish it. An' I wish I'd ha' married 'er.

MRS PURDY: Come, my lad, come. Married tha art –

LUTHER [*bitterly*]: Married I am, an' I wish I worna. Your Bertha 'er'd 'a thought a thousand times more on me than *she* does. But I'm wrong, wrong, wrong, i' ivry breath I take. An' I will be wrong, yi, an' I *will* be wrong.

MRS PURDY: Hush thee – there's somebody comin'.

[*They wait. Enter* JOE *and* MINNIE, JOE *talking loudly.*]

MINNIE: No, you've not, you've no right at all. [*To* LUTHER]: Haven't you even cleared away? [*To* MRS PURDY]: Good evening.

MRS PURDY: Good evenin', missis. I was just goin' – I've bin sayin' it looks very nice, th' 'ouse.

MINNIE: Do you think so?

MRS PURDY: I do, indeed.

MINNIE: Don't notice of the mess we're in, shall you? *He* [*pointing to* JOE] broke the plates – and then I had to rush off up to Mrs Preston's afore I could clear away. And he hasn't even mended the fire.

LUTHER: I can do – I niver noticed.

MINNIE [*to* MRS PURDY]: Have a piece of cake? [*Goes to cupboard.*]

MRS PURDY: No, thanks, no, thanks. I mun get off afore th' Co-op shuts up. Thank yer very much. Well – good night, all.

[JOE *opens the door;* MRS PURDY *goes out.*]

MINNIE [*bustling, clearing away as* LUTHER *comes in with coals*]:
Did you settle it?

LUTHER: What?

MINNIE: What she'd come about.

LUTHER: Ah.

MINNIE: An' I bet you'll go and forget.

LUTHER: Oh ah!

MINNIE: And poor old Bob Purdy will go on just the same.

LUTHER: Very likely.

MINNIE: Don't let the dust all go on the hearth. Why didn't
you clear away? The house was like a pigsty for her to come
into.

LUTHER: Then I wor the pig.

MINNIE [*halting*]: Why – who's trod on your tail now?

LUTHER: There'd be nobody to tread on it if tha wor out.

MINNIE: Oh – oh, dearo' me. [*To* JOE]: I think we'd better go
to the Cinematograph, and leave him to nurse his sore tail.

JOE: We better had.

LUTHER: An' joy go with yer.

MINNIE: We certainly shan't leave it at home. [*To* JOE]: What
time does it begin?

JOE: Seven o'clock.

MINNIE: And I want to call in Sisson's shop. Shall you go
with me, or wouldn't you condescend to go shopping with
me? [*She has cleared the table, brought a tray and a bowl, and is
washing up the pots.*]

JOE: Dost think I'm daunted by Polly Sisson?

MINNIE: You're braver than most men if you dare go in a
shop. Here, take a towel and wipe these pots.

JOE: How can I?

MINNIE: If you were a gentleman, you'd hold the plates in
your teeth to wipe them.

JOE: Tha wouldna look very ladylike at th' end on't.

MINNIE: Why?

JOE: Why, hast forgot a'ready, what a shine tha kicked up
when I broke them two other plates? [*He has got a towel, and
wedging a plate against his thighs, is laboriously wiping it.*]

MINNIE: I never kicked up a shine. It *is* nice of you!

114

JOE: What?

MINNIE: To do this for me.

[LUTHER *has begun sweeping the hearth.*]

JOE: Tha's got two servants.

MINNIE: But I'm sure you want to smoke while you're doing it – don't you now?

JOE: Sin' tha says so. [*Fumbles in his pocket.*]

MINNIE [*hastily wiping her hands, puts a cigarette between his lips – gets matches from the mantelpiece, ignoring her husband, who is kneeling sweeping the hearth – lights his cigarette*]: It's so nice to have a lamed man. You feel you've got an excuse for making a fuss of him. You've got awfully nice eyes and eyebrows. I like dark eyes.

JOE: Oh ah!

[LUTHER *rises hastily, goes in the passage, crosses the room quietly. He wears his coat, a red scarf and a cap.*]

MINNIE: There's more go in them than in blue. [*Watches her husband go out. There is silence between the two.*]

JOE: He'll come round again.

MINNIE: He'll have to. He'll go on sulking now. [*Her face breaks.*] You – you don't know how hard it is.

JOE: What?

MINNIE [*crying a few fierce tears*]: This . . .

JOE [*aghast*]: What?

MINNIE: Why – you don't know. You don't know how hard it is, with a man as – as leaves you alone all the time.

JOE: But – he niver hardly goes out.

MINNIE: No, but – you don't know – he leaves me alone, he always has done – and there's nobody . . .

JOE: But he . . .

MINNIE: He never trusts me – he leaves me so alone – and – [*a little burst of tears*] it *is* hard! [*She changes suddenly.*] You've wiped your plates; my word, you are a champion.

JOE: I think so an' a'.

MINNIE: I hope the pictures will be jolly – but the sad ones make me laugh more, don't they you?

JOE: I canna do wi' 'em.

CURTAIN

ACT TWO

The same evening – eleven o'clock. LUTHER'S *house.*

MINNIE, *alone, weeping. She gets up, fills the kettle, puts it on the hob, sits down, weeps again; then hears somebody coming, dries her eyes swiftly, turns the lamp low.*

Enter LUTHER. *He stands in the doorway – is rather tipsy; flings his cap down, sits in his chair, lurching it slightly. Neither speaks for some moments.*

LUTHER: Well, did yer like yer pictures?

MINNIE: Where have you been?

LUTHER: What does it matter where I've been?

MINNIE: Have you been drinking?

LUTHER: What's it matter if I have?

MINNIE: It matters a lot to me.

LUTHER: Oh ah!

MINNIE: Do you think I'm going to sleep with a man who is half-drunk?

LUTHER: Nay, I non know who tha'rt goin' ter sleep wi'.

MINNIE [*rising*]: I shall make the bed in the other room.

LUTHER: Tha's no 'casions. I s'll do very nicely on t' sofa; it's warmer.

MINNIE: Oh, you can have your own bed.

LUTHER: If tha doesna sleep in it, I dunna.

MINNIE: And if *you do*, I don't.

LUTHER: Tha pleases thysen. Tha can sleep by thysen for iver, if ter's a mind to't.

MINNIE [*who has stood hesitating*]: Oh, very well! [*She goes upstairs, returns immediately with a pillow and two blankets, which she throws on the sofa.*]

LUTHER: Thank yer kindly.

MINNIE: Shall you rake?

LUTHER: I'll rake.

[*She moves about; lays table for his morning's breakfast: a newspaper, cup, plate, etc. – no food, because it would go*

116

dry; rinses his tin pit-bottle, puts it and his snap-bag on the table.]

I could do it for mysen. Tha ned do nowt for me.

MINNIE: Why this sudden fit of unselfishness?

LUTHER: I niver want thee to do nowt for me, niver no more. No, not so much as lift a finger for me – not if I wor dyin'.

MINNIE: You're not dying; you're only tipsy.

LUTHER: Well, it's no matter to thee what I am.

MINNIE: It's very comfortable for you to think so.

LUTHER: I know nowt about that.

MINNIE [*after a pause*]: Where have you been to-night?

LUTHER: There an' back, to see how far it is.

MINNIE [*making an effort*]: Have you been up to your mother's?

LUTHER: Where I've bin, I've bin, and where I haven't, I haven't.

MINNIE: Pah! – you needn't try to magnify it and make a mountain. You've been to your mother's, and then to 'The Ram.'

LUTHER: All right – if tha knows, tha knows, an' theer's an end on't.

MINNIE: You talk like a fool.

LUTHER: That comes o' bein' a fool.

MINNIE: When were you a fool?

LUTHER: Ivry day o' my life, an' ivry breath I've ta'en.

MINNIE [*having finished work, sits down again*]: I suppose you haven't got it in you to say anything fresh.

LUTHER: Why, what dost want me ter say? [*He looks at her for the first time.*]

MINNIE [*with a queer catch*]: You might be more of a man if you said you were sorry.

LUTHER: Sorry! Sorry for what?

MINNIE: You've nothing to be sorry *for*, have you?

LUTHER [*looking at her, quickly*]: What art goin' ter say?

MINNIE: It's what are *you* going to say. [*A silence.*]

LUTHER [*doggedly*]: I'm goin' ter say nowt.

MINNIE [*bitterly*]: No, you're not *man* enough to say anything – you can only slobber. You do a woman a wrong, but you're

never man enough to say you're sorry for it. You're *not* a
man, you're not – you're something crawling!

LUTHER: I'm glad! I'm glad! I'm glad! No, an' I wouldna
ta'e't back, no. 'Er wor nice wi' me, which is a thing tha's
niver bin. An' so tha's got it, an' mun keep it.

MINNIE: Who was nice with you?

LUTHER: *She* was – an' would ha'e bin at this minnit, but for
thee.

MINNIE: Pah! – you're not fit to have a wife. You only want
your mother to rock you to sleep.

LUTHER: Neither mother, nor wife, neither thee nor onybody
do I want – no – no.

MINNIE: No – you've had three cans of beer.

LUTHER: An' if ter niver sleeps i' th' bed wi' me again, an' if
ter niver does a hand's turn for me niver no more, I'm glad,
I'm glad. I non want thee. I non want ter see thee.

MINNIE: You mean coward. Good God! I never thought you
were such a mean coward as this.

LUTHER: An' as for thy money – yi, I wouldna smell on't.
An' neither thine, nor our Joe's, nor my mother's will I
ha'e. What I addle's my own. What I gi'e thee, I gi'e thee.
An' she maun ha'e ten shillin's a month, an' tha maun abide
by't.

MINNIE: What are you talking about?

LUTHER: My mother wouldna gi'e me th' money. She says
she's done her share. An' tha's done thine. An' I've done
mine, begod. An' what yer canna chew yer maun swaller.

MINNIE: You must be quite drunk.

LUTHER: Must I? Alright, it's Dutch courage then. A'right,
then Dutch courage it is. But I tell thee, tha does as ter's a
mind. Tha can leave me, an' go back inter service, if ter
wants. What's it ter me, if I'm but a lump o' suck i' th'
'ouse wheer tha art? Tha should ha' had our Joe – he's got
more go than me. An' I should ha' had 'er. I'd got go
enough for *her*; 'appen a bit too much.

MINNIE: Her? Who?

LUTHER: Her! An' I'm glad 'er's wi' my childt. I'm glad I
did it. I'm glad! For tha's wiped tha feet on me enough. Yi,

tha's wiped thy feet on me till what's it to me if tha does it
or not? It isna! An' now – tha maun abide by what ter's
got, tha maun. I s'll ha'e to – an' by plenty I hadna got I've
abided. An' so – an' so – yi.

MINNIE: But who is it you – who is she?

LUTHER: Tha knowed a' along.

MINNIE: Who is it?

　　[*They are both silent.*]

　Aren't you going to speak?

LUTHER: What's the good?

MINNIE [*coldly*]: But I must know.

LUTHER: Tha does know.

MINNIE: I can assure you I don't.

LUTHER: Then assure thysen an' find out.

　　[*Another silence.*]

MINNIE: Do you mean somebody is going to have a baby by
you?

LUTHER: I mean what I've said, an' I mean nowt else.

MINNIE: But you must tell me.

LUTHER: I've boiled my cabbage twice a'ready, hanna I?

MINNIE: Do you mean somebody is going to have a child
by you?

LUTHER: Tha can chew it ower, if ter's a mind.

MINNIE [*helpless*]: But . . . [*She struggles with herself, then goes
calm.*]

LUTHER: That's what I say – *but* . . . !

　　[*A silence.*]

MINNIE: And who is she?

LUTHER: Thee, for a' I know.

MINNIE [*calmly, patiently*]: I asked you a question.

LUTHER: Ah – an' I 'eered thee.

MINNIE: Then answer me – who is she?

LUTHER: Tha knows well enow – tha knowed afore they'd
towd thee –

MINNIE: Nobody has told me. Who is she?

LUTHER: Well, tha's seed 'er mother.

MINNIE [*numb*]: Mrs Purdy?

LUTHER: Yi.

MINNIE: Their Bertha?

LUTHER: Yi.

[*A silence.*]

MINNIE: Why didn't you tell me?

LUTHER: Tell thee what?

MINNIE: This.

LUTHER: Tha knowed afore I did.

MINNIE: I know *now*.

LUTHER: Me an' a'.

[*A pause.*]

MINNIE: Didn't you know till to-night?

LUTHER: Our Joe told me when tha'd just gone – I niver dreamt afore – an' then 'er mother . . .

MINNIE: What did her mother come for?

LUTHER: Ter see if we could hush it up a'cause o' thee, an' gi'e 'er a lump sum.

MINNIE: Hush it up because of me?

LUTHER: Ah – lay it ont'r an electrician as wor wi' th' gang as laid th' cable down to Balford – he's gone God knows where.

MINNIE: But it's yours.

LUTHER: I know that.

MINNIE: Then why lay it onto somebody else?

LUTHER: Because o' thee.

MINNIE: But why because of me?

LUTHER: To stop thee knowin', I s'd think.

MINNIE: And why shouldn't I know?

LUTHER: Eh, I dunno.

[*A pause.*]

MINNIE: And what were you going to do to stop me knowing?

LUTHER: 'Er axed for forty pounds down.

MINNIE: And if you paid forty pounds, you got off scot-free?

LUTHER: Summat so.

MINNIE: And where were the forty pounds coming from?

LUTHER: Our Joe said 'e'd lend 'em me. I thought my mother would, but 'er said 'er wouldna – neither would she gi'e't our Joe ter lend me, she said. For I wor a married

man now, an' it behoved my wife to look after me. An' I
thought tha knowed. I thought tha'd twigged, else bin
telled. An' I didna care, an' dunna care.

MINNIE: And this is what you married me to!

LUTHER: This is what tha married me to. But I'll niver ax
thee for, no, not so much as the liftin' of a finger – no –

MINNIE: But when you wrote and told me you were willing
to marry me, why didn't you tell me this?

LUTHER: Because – as I've telled thee – I didna know till
this very mortal night.

MINNIE: But you knew you'd been with her.

LUTHER: Ay, I knowed that.

  [*A pause.*]

MINNIE: And why didn't you tell me?

LUTHER: What for should I tell thee? What good would it
ha' done thee? Tha niver towd *me* nowt.

MINNIE: So that is how you look at it?

LUTHER: I non care how I look at it.

  [*A pause.*]

MINNIE: And was there anybody else?

LUTHER: How dost mean?

MINNIE: Have you been with any other woman?

LUTHER: I dunno – I might – I dunno.

MINNIE: That means you have.

LUTHER: I'm thirty.

MINNIE: And who *were* they?

LUTHER: I dunno. I've niver bin much wi' anybody – little,
very little – an' then it wor an off-chance. Our Joe wor more
that way than me – I worn't that way.

  [*A pause.*]

MINNIE: So – this was what I waited for you for!

LUTHER: Tha niver waited for me. Tha had me a'cause tha
couldna get nobody better.

MINNIE: And so –

LUTHER [*after a moment*]: Yi, an' so. An' so, I non care what
ter does. If ter leaves me –

MINNIE [*in a flash*]: What's the good of me leaving you?
Aren't I married to you – tied to you?

LUTHER: Tha could leave me whether or not. I should go t'r
Australia wi' our Joe.

MINNIE: And what about that girl?

LUTHER: I should send 'er th' money.

MINNIE: And what about me?

LUTHER: Tha'd please thysen.

MINNIE: Should you *like* me to leave you, and let you go to
Australia?

LUTHER: 'Appen I should.

MINNIE: What did you marry me for?

LUTHER: 'Cos tha axed me.

MINNIE: Did you never care for me?

[*He does not answer.*]

Didn't you?

[*He does not answer.*]

Didn't you?

LUTHER [*slowly*]: You niver wanted me – you thought me
dirt.

MINNIE: Ha! [*A pause.*] You can have the forty pounds.

LUTHER [*very doggedly*]: I shanna.

MINNIE: She's got to be paid.

LUTHER: Tha keeps thy money.

MINNIE: Then where shall you get it from?

LUTHER: I s'll pay 'er month by month.

MINNIE: But you can't. Think!

LUTHER: Then I'll borrow forty quid somewhere else, an'
pay it back i' instalments. Tha keeps thy money.

MINNIE: You can borrow it from me.

LUTHER: I shall not.

MINNIE: Very well. I only wanted not to have the bother of
paying month by month. I think I shall go back to my old
place.

LUTHER: Tha pleases thysen.

MINNIE: And you can go and live with your mother again.

LUTHER: That I should niver do – but tha pleases thysen.
We've bin married seven wik come Tuesday.

MINNIE: I niver ought to ha' done it.

LUTHER: What?

MINNIE: Married you.

LUTHER: No.

MINNIE: For you never cared enough.

LUTHER: Yi – it's my fault.

MINNIE: Yes.

LUTHER: It would be. Tha's niver made a fault i' thy life.

MINNIE: Who are you, to talk about my faults!

LUTHER: Well –

[*A pause.*]

MINNIE: I shall write to Mr Westlake to-morrow.

LUTHER: Tha does as pleases thee.

MINNIE: And if they can't take me back straight away, I shall ask him if he knows another place.

LUTHER: A'right. An' we'll sell th' furniture.

MINNIE [*looking round at her home*]: Yes.

LUTHER: It'll non bring ha'ef tha giv for't – but it'll bring enough ter ta'e me out theer.

MINNIE: I'll make up what you lose by it, since I chose it.

LUTHER: Tha can give ter them as'll ha'e.

MINNIE: But I shall feel I owe it you.

LUTHER: I've had six weeks o' married life wi' thee. I mun pay for that.

MINNIE: You are mean, mean.

LUTHER: I know – though tha'rt first as has told me so. When dost reckon tha'lt go?

MINNIE: I'll go to-morrow if you want to get rid of me.

LUTHER: Nay – tha does just as pleases thysen. I non want ter get rid on thee. Nay, nay, it's not that. It's thee as wants ter go.

MINNIE: At any rate, I s'll have a place inside a fortnight.

LUTHER [*dully*]: Alright.

MINNIE: So I shall have to trouble you till then.

LUTHER: But I dunna want thee ter do owt for me – no, I dunna.

MINNIE: I shall keep the house, in payment for my board and lodgings. And I'll make the bed up in the back room, and I'll sleep there, because it's not furnished, and the house is yours.

LUTHER: Th'art – th'art – I wish I might strike thee down!

MINNIE: And I shall keep the account of every penny I spend, and you must just pay the bills.

LUTHER [*rising suddenly*]: I'll murder thee afore tha does.

[*He goes out. She sits twisting her apron. He returns with a large lump of coal in his hands, and rakes the fire.*]

MINNIE: You cared more for her than for me.

LUTHER: For who?

MINNIE: For her. She was the sort of sawney you ought to have had. Did she think you perfect?

LUTHER [*with grim satisfaction*]: She liked me.

MINNIE: And you could do just as you wanted with her?

LUTHER: She'd ha' done owt for me.

MINNIE: And it flattered you, did it? Because a long stalk wi' no flower was at your service, it flattered you, did it? My word, it ought – As for your Joe, he's not a fool like you, and that's why women think more of him. He wouldn't want a Bertha Purdy. He'd get a woman who was something – and because he knew how to appreciate her. You – what good are you?

LUTHER: I'm no good, but to fetch an' carry.

MINNIE: And a tuppenny scullery-girl could do that as well.

LUTHER: Alright.

MINNIE: I'll bet even Bertha Purdy thinks what a clown you are. She never wanted you to marry her, did she?

LUTHER: She knowed I wouldn't.

MINNIE: You flatter yourself. I'll bet she never wanted you. I shouldn't be surprised if the child isn't somebody else's, that she just foists on you because you're so soft.

LUTHER: Oh ah!

MINNIE: It even flatters you to think it's yours.

LUTHER: Oh ah!

MINNIE: And quite right too – for it's the only thing you could have to be proud of. And then really it's not you ...

LUTHER: Oh ah!

MINNIE: If a woman has a child, and you think you're the cause, do you think it's *your* doings?

LUTHER: If tha has one, it will be.

MINNIE: And is *that* anything for you to be proud of? Me whom you've insulted and deceived and treated as no snail would treat a woman! And then you expect me to bear your children!

LUTHER: I dunna expect thee. If tha does tha does.

MINNIE: And you gloat over it and feel proud of it!

LUTHER: Yi, I do.

MINNIE: No – no! I'd rather have married a tramp off the streets than you. And – and I don't believe you *can* have children.

LUTHER: Theer tha knows tha'rt a liar.

MINNIE: I hate you.

LUTHER: Alright.

MINNIE: And I *will* leave you, I *will*.

LUTHER: Tha's said so afore.

MINNIE: And I mean it.

LUTHER: Alright.

MINNIE: But it's your mother's doing. *She* mollycoddled and marded you till you weren't a man – and now – I have to pay for it.

LUTHER: Oh ah!

MINNIE: No, you're not a man!

LUTHER: Alright. They's plenty of women as would say I am.

MINNIE: They'd be lying to get something out of you.

LUTHER: Why, what could they get outer me?

MINNIE: Yes – yes – what could they . . . [*She stutters to a close.*] [*He begins to take off his boots.*]

LUTHER: If tha'rt goin', tha'd better go afore th' strike begins. We should be on short commons then – ten bob a wik.

MINNIE: There's one thing, you'd be on short commons without me. For nobody would keep you for ten shillings a week, unless you went to your mother's.

LUTHER: I could live at our Harriet's, an' pay 'er off after. An' there'd be th' furniture sold.

MINNIE: And you'd be delighted if there *was* a strike, so you could loaf about. You don't even get drunk. You only loaf.

You're lazy, lazy, and without the stomach of a louse. You *want* a strike.

LUTHER: Alright.

MINNIE: And I hope you'll get what you deserve, I do.

LUTHER: Tha'rt gi'en it me.

MINNIE [*lifting her hand suddenly*]: How *dare* you say so – how *dare* you! I'm too good for you.

LUTHER [*sullenly*]: I know.

MINNIE: Yes. [*She gets a candle, lights it, and goes to bed. He flings off his scarf and coat and waistcoat, throws the pillow on the hearthrug, wraps himself in the blankets, blows the lamp out, and lies down.*]

CURTAIN

ACT THREE

A fortnight later — afternoon. The kitchen of LUTHER
GASCOIGNE'S *house.*

MRS GASCOIGNE, *senior, alone. Enter* MINNIE GASCOIGNE,
dressed from travelling. She is followed by a CABMAN *carrying
a bag.*

MRS GASCOIGNE: What — is it you!

MINNIE: Yes. Didn't you get my wire?

MRS GASCOIGNE: Thy wire! Dost mean a tallygram? No,
    we'n had nowt though th' house 'as bin shut up.

MINNIE [*to the* CABMAN]: Thank you. How much?

CABMAN: Ha'ef-a-crown.

MRS GASCOIGNE: Ha'ef-a-crown for commin' from th'
    Midland station! Why, tha non know what's talkin' about.

MINNIE [*paying him*]: Thank you.

CABMAN: Thank yer. Good afternoon.

    [*The* CABMAN *goes out.*]

MRS GASCOIGNE: My word, tha knows how ter ma'e th'
    money fly.

MINNIE: I couldn't carry a bag.

MRS GASCOIGNE: Tha could ha' come i' th' 'bus ter East-
    wood an' then a man 'ud 'a browt it on.

MINNIE: It is raining.

MRS GASCOIGNE: Tha'rt neither sugar nor salt.

MINNIE: I wonder you didn't get my telegram.

MRS GASCOIGNE: I tell thee, th' 'ouse wor shut up last night.

MINNIE: Oh!

MRS GASCOIGNE: I dunno wheer 'e slep' — wi' some o's pals
    I should think.

MINNIE: Oh!

MRS GASCOIGNE: Thinks I to mysen, I'd better go an' get
    some dinner ready down theer. So I told our Joe ter come
    'ere for's dinner as well, but they'm neither on 'em bin in
    yet. That's allers t'road when it's strike. They stop mormin'

about, bletherin' and boomin' an' meals, bless yer, they don't count. Tha's bin i' Manchester four days then?

MINNIE: Yes.

MRS GASCOIGNE: Ay. – Our Luther's niver bin up ter tell me. If I hadna ha' met Mrs Pervin fra next door here, I should niver ha' knowed a word. That wor yisterday. So I sent our Joe down. But it seems 'e's neither bin a-whoam yesterday nor th' day afore. He slep' i' th' 'ouse by hissen for two nights. So Mrs Sharley said. He said tha'd gone ter Manchester on business.

MINNIE: Yes.

MRS GASCOIGNE: But he niver come ter tell *me* nowt on't.

MINNIE: Didn't he?

MRS GASCOIGNE: It's trew what they say:

  'My son's my son till he ta'es him a wife,
    But my daughter's my daughter the whole of her life.'

MINNIE: Do you think so?

MRS GASCOIGNE: I'm sure. An' th' men's been out ten days now, an' such carryin's-on.

MINNIE: Oh! Why – what?

MRS GASCOIGNE: Meetin's ivry mornin' – crier for ever down th' street wi's bell – an' agitators. They say as Fraser dursn't venture out o' th' door. Watna' pit-top's bin afire, and there's a rigiment o' soldiers drillin' i' th' statutes ground – bits o' things they are, an' a', like a lot o' little monkeys i' their red coats – Staffordshire men. But wiry, so they say. Same as marched wi' Lord Roberts to Candyhar. But not a man among 'em. If you watch out fra th' gardin end, you'll see 'em i' th' colliers' train goin' up th' line ter Watna' – wi' their red coats jammed i' th' winders. They say as Fraser's got ten on 'em in's house ter guard him – an' they's sentinels at pit top, standin' wi' their guns, an' th' men crackin' their sides wi' laughing at 'em.

MINNIE: What for?

MRS GASCOIGNE: Nay, that I canna tell thee. They've got the Black Watch up at Heanor – so they says – great big Scotchmen i' kilts. They look well, ha'en them i' Heanor, wi' a' them lasses.

MINNIE: And what is all the fuss about?

MRS GASCOIGNE: Riotin'. I thought tha'd bobbled off ter Manchester ter be i' safety.

MINNIE: Oh, no – I never knew there was any danger.

MRS GASCOIGNE: No more there is, as far as that goes. What's up atween you an' our Luther?

MINNIE: Oh, nothing particular.

MRS GASCOIGNE: I knowed summat wor amiss, when 'e niver come up. It's a fortnight last Tuesday, sin' 'e's set foot i' my house – an' I've niver clapt eyes on him. I axed our Joe, but he's as stubborn as a jackass, an' you canna get a word out on 'im, not for love nor money.

MINNIE: Oh!

MRS GASCOIGNE: Talks o' goin' t'r Australay. But not if I can help it. An' hints as if our Luther – you not thinkin' of it, are you?

MINNIE: No, I'm not – not that I know of.

MRS GASCOIGNE: H'm! It's a rum go, when nobody seems ter know where they are, nor what they're goin' ter do. But there's more blort than bustle, i' this world. What took thee to Manchester?

MINNIE: Oh, I just wanted to go, on business.

MRS GASCOIGNE: Summat about thy money, like?

MINNIE: Yes.

MRS GASCOIGNE: Our Luther wor axin' me for forty pound, th' last time 'e wor up – but I didna see it. No – I fun' him a' as 'e wanted for's marriage, and gen 'im ten pound i' hand, an' I thought it 'ud suffice. An' as for forty pound – it's ter much, that's what I think.

MINNIE: I don't.

MRS GASCOIGNE: Oh, well, if tha doesna, a' well an' good. 'Appen he's paid it, then?

MINNIE: Paid it! Why, wheer was he to get it from?

MRS GASCOIGNE: I thought you had it atween you.

MINNIE: We haven't.

MRS GASCOIGNE: Why, how dost mean?

MINNIE: I mean we've neither of us got as much as forty pounds.

MRS GASCOIGNE: Dost mean *tha* hasna?

MINNIE: No, I haven't.

MRS GASCOIGNE: What's a-gait now?

MINNIE: Nothing.

MRS GASCOIGNE: What hast bin up to?

MINNIE: I? Nothing. I went to Manchester to settle a little business, that's all.

MRS GASCOIGNE: And wheer did ter stop?

MINNIE: I stayed with my old master.

MRS GASCOIGNE: Wor there no missis, then?

MINNIE: No – his wife is dead. You know I was governess for his grandchildren, who were born in India.

MRS GASCOIGNE: H'm! So tha went to see *him*?

MINNIE: Yes – I've always told him everything.

MRS GASCOIGNE: So tha went clat-fartin' ter 'im about our Luther, did ter?

MINNIE: Well – he's the only soul in the world that I *can* go to.

MRS GASCOIGNE: H'm! It doesna become thee, methinks.

MINNIE: Well!

[*Footsteps are heard.*]

MRS GASCOIGNE: Here's them lads, I s'd think.

[*Enter* LUTHER *and* JOE.]

JOE [*to* MINNIE]: Hello! has thee come?

MINNIE: Yes. I sent a wire, and thought someone might come to meet me.

JOE: Nay, there wor no wire. We thought tha'd gone for good.

MINNIE: Who thought so?

JOE: Well – didna tha say so?

MINNIE: Say what?

JOE: As tha'd go, an' he could do what he liked?

MINNIE: I've said many things.

MRS GASCOIGNE: So that was how it stood! Tha'rt a fool, our Luther. If ter ta'es a woman at 'er word, well, tha deserves what ter gets.

LUTHER: What am I to do, might I ax?

MRS GASCOIGNE: Nay, that thy wits should tell thee. Wheer hast bin these two days?

LUTHER: I walked ower wi' Jim Horrocks ter their Annie's i' Mansfield.

MRS GASCOIGNE: I'm sure she'd got enough to do, without two men planting themselves on her. An' how did ter get back?

LUTHER: Walked.

MRS GASCOIGNE: Trapsein' thy shoe-leather off thee feet, walkin' twenty miles. Hast had thy dinner?

JOE: We've both had free dinners at th' Methodist Chapel.

LUTHER: I met Tom Heseldine i' 'Th' Badger Box', Mother.

MRS GASCOIGNE: Oh ay! Wide-mouthed as iver, I reckon.

JOE: Just same. But what dost think, Mother? It's leaked out as Fraser's got a lot o' chaps to go to-morrer mornin', ter see after th' roads an' a' that.

MRS GASCOIGNE: Th' roads wants keepin' safe, dunna they?

JOE: Yi – but if th' mesters wunna ha'e th' union men, let 'em do it theirselves.

MRS GASCOIGNE: Tha talks like a fool.

LUTHER: What right ha' they ter get a lot of scrawdrags an' blacklegs in ter do our work? A' th' pit maun fa' in, if they wunna settle it fair wi' us.

JOE: Then workin's is ours, an' th' mesters'. If th' mesters wunna treat us fair, then they mun keep 'em right theirselves. They non goin' ter ha'e no third body in.

MINNIE: But even when it's settled, how are you going back, if the roof has come in, and the roads are gone?

JOE: Tha mun ax th' mesters that. If we canna go back ter th' rotten owd pits no more, we mun look elsewhere. An' th' mesters can sit atop o' their pits an' stroke 'em.

LUTHER [to MINNIE]: If I got a woman in to do th' house-work as tha wunna do for me, tha'd sit smilin', shouldn't ter?

MINNIE: She could do as she liked.

LUTHER: Alright. Then, Mother, 'appen tha'lt boss this house. She run off ter Manchester, an' left me ter starve. So 'appen tha'lt come an' do for me.

MRS GASCOIGNE: Nay – if ter wants owt tha mun come ter *me*.

JOE: That's right. Dunna thee play blackleg i' this establishment.

MRS GASCOIGNE: I s'll mind my own business.

JOE [*to* MINNIE]: Now, does *thee* think it right, Minnie, as th' mesters should get a lot o' crawlin' buggers in ter keep their pits i' order, when th' keepin' o' them pits i' order belongs by right to us?

MINNIE: It belongs to whosoever the masters pay to do it.

LUTHER: A' right. Then it belongs to me to ha'e any woman in ter do for me, as I've a mind. Tha's gone on strike, so I ha'e the right ter get anybody else.

MINNIE: When have I gone on strike? I have always done your housework.

LUTHER: Housework – yi! But we dunna on'y keep th' roof from comin' in. We *get* as well. An' even th' housework tha went on strike wi'. Tha skedaddled off ter Manchester, an' left me to't.

MINNIE: I went on business.

LUTHER: An' we've come out on strike 'on business'.

MINNIE: You've not; it's a game.

LUTHER: An' the mesters'll ta'e us back when they're ready, or when they're forced to. An' same wi' thee by me.

MINNIE: Oh!

JOE: We got it fr' Tom Rooke – 'e wor goin' ter turn 'em down. At four to-morrer mornin', there's ower twenty men goin' down.

MRS GASCOIGNE: What a lot of fools men are! As if th' pits didn't need ter be kep' tidy, ready for you to go back to'm.

JOE: They'll be kep' tidy by us, then an' when we've a mind – an' by nobody else.

MRS GASCOIGNE: Tha talks very high an' mighty. That's because I ha'e th' feedin' on thee.

JOE: You put it like our Luther says, then. He stands for t'mesters, an' Minnie stands for t'men – cos 'er's gone on strike. Now becos she's went ter Manchester, had he got ony right ter ha'e Lizzie Charley in for a couple o' nights an' days?

MRS GASCOIGNE: Tha talks like a fool!

JOE: I dunna.

MINNIE: He's welcome to Lizzie Charley.

JOE: Alright. – She's a nice gel. We'll ax 'er to come in an' manage th' 'ouse – he can pay 'er.

MINNIE: What with?

JOE: Niver you mind. Should yer like it?

MINNIE: He can do just as he likes.

JOE: Then should I fetch her? – should I, Luther?

LUTHER: If ter's a mind.

JOE: Should I, then, Minnie?

MINNIE: If he wants her.

LUTHER: I want somebody ter look after me.

JOE: Right tha art. [*Puts his cap on.*] I'll say as Minnie canna look after th' house, will 'er come. That it?

LUTHER: Ah.

MRS GASCOIGNE: Dunna be a fool. Tha's had a can or two.

JOE: Well – 'er'll be glad o' the job.

MRS GASCOIGNE: You'd better stop him, one of you.

LUTHER: I want somebody ter look after me – an' tha wunna.

MRS GASCOIGNE: Eh dear o' me! Dunna thee be a fool our Joe.

    [*Exit* JOE.]

What wor this job about goin' ter Manchester?

LUTHER: She said she wouldna live wi' me, an' so 'er went. I thought 'er'd gone for good.

MINNIE: You didn't – you *knew*.

LUTHER: I knowed what tha'd towd me – as tha'd live wi' me no longer. Tha's come back o' thy own accord.

MINNIE: I never said I shouldn't come back.

LUTHER: Tha said as tha wouldna live wi' me. An' tha *didna*, neither, – not for –

MRS GASCOIGNE: Well, Minnie, you've brought it on your own head. You put him off, an' you put him off, as if 'e was of no account, an' then all of a sudden you invited him to marry you –

MINNIE: Put him off! He didn't need much putting off. He never came any faster than a snail.

MRS GASCOIGNE: Twice, to my knowledge, he axed thee – an' what can a man do more?

133

MINNIE: Yes, what! A gramophone in breeches could do as much.

MRS GASCOIGNE: Oh, indeed! What ailed him was, he wor in collier's britches, i'stead o' a stool-arsed Jack's.

MINNIE: No – what ailed him was that *you* kept him like a kid hanging on to you.

MRS GASCOIGNE: An' tha bit thy own nose off, when ter said him nay. For had ter married him at twenty-three, there'd ha' been none of this trouble.

MINNIE: And why didn't I? Why didn't I? Because he came in his half-hearted 'I will if you like' fashion, and I despised him, yes I did.

MRS GASCOIGNE: And who are *you* to be despising him, I should like to know?

MINNIE: I'm a woman, and that's enough. But I know now, it was your fault. You held him, and persuaded him that what he wanted was *you*. You kept him, like a child, you even gave him what money he wanted, like a child. He never roughed it – he never faced out anything. You did all that for him.

MRS GASCOIGNE: And what if I did! If you made as good a wife to him as I made a mother, you'd do.

MINNIE: Should I? You didn't care what women your sons went with, so long as they didn't love them. What do you care really about this affair of Bertha Purdy? You don't. All you cared about was to keep your sons for yourself. You kept the solid meal, and the orts and slarts any other woman could have. But I tell you, I'm *not* for having the orts and slarts, and your leavings from your sons. I'll have a man, or nothing, I will.

MRS GASCOIGNE: It's rare to be some folks, ter pick and choose.

MINNIE: I can't pick and choose, no. But what I won't have, I won't have, and that is all.

MRS GASCOIGNE [*to* LUTHER]: Have I ever kept thee from doin' as tha wanted? Have I iver marded and coddled thee?

LUTHER: Tha hasna, beguy!

MINNIE: No, you haven't, perhaps, not by the look of things.

But you've bossed him. You've decided everything for him, really. He's depended on you as much when he was thirty as when he was three. You told him what to do, and he did it.

MRS GASCOIGNE: My word, I've never known all he did.

MINNIE: You have – everything that mattered. You maybe didn't know it was Bertha Purdy, but you knew it was some woman like her, and what did you care? *She* had the orts and slarts, you kept your son. And you want to keep him, even now. Yes – and you do keep him.

MRS GASCOIGNE: We're learnin' a thing or two, Luther.

LUTHER: Ay.

[*Enter* JOE.]

MINNIE: Yes! What did you care about the woman who would have to take some after you? Nothing! You left her with just the slarts of a man. Yes.

MRS GASCOIGNE: Indeed! I canna see as you're so badly off. You've got a husband as doesn't drink, as waits on you hand and foot, as gives you a free hand in everything. It's you as doesn't know when you're well off, madam.

MINNIE: I'd rather have had a husband who knocked me about than a husband who was good to me because he belonged to his mother. He doesn't and can't *really* care for me. You stand before him. His *real* caring goes to *you*. Me he only wants sometimes.

JOE: She'll be in in a minute.

MRS GASCOIGNE: Tha'rt the biggest fool an' jackanapes, our Joe, as iver God made.

MINNIE: If she crosses that doorstep, then I go for good.

MRS GASCOIGNE [*bursting into fury – to* JOE]: Tha see what thy bobby interferin' has done.

JOE: Nay – that's how it stood.

MRS GASCOIGNE: Tha mun go an' stop her, our Luther. Tell 'er it wor our Joe's foolery. An' look sharp.

LUTHER: What should *I* go for?

[LUTHER *goes out, furious.*]

MINNIE: You see – you see! His mother's word is law to him. He'd do what I told him, but his *feel* would be for you. He's got no *feeling* for me. You keep all that.

MRS GASCOIGNE: You talk like a jealous woman.

MINNIE: I do! And for that matter, why doesn't Joe marry, either? Because you keep him too. You know, in spite of his bluster, he cares more for your little finger than he does for all the women in the world – or ever will. And it's wrong – it's wrong. How is a woman ever to have a husband, when the men all belong to their mothers? It's wrong.

MRS GASCOIGNE: Oh, indeed! – is it? You know, don't you? You know everything.

MINNIE: I know this, because I've suffered from it. Your elder sons you let go, and they *are* husbands. But your young sons you've kept. And Luther is your son, and the man that lives with me. But first, he's your son. And Joe ought never to marry, for he'd break a woman's heart.

MRS GASCOIGNE: Tha hears, lad! We're bein' told off.

JOE: Ah, I hear. An' what's more, it's true, Mother.

MINNIE: It is – it is. He only likes playing round me and getting some pleasure out of teasing me, because he knows I'm safely married to Luther, and can never look to him to marry me and belong to me. He's safe, so he likes me. If I were single, he'd be frightened to death of me.

JOE: Happen I should.

MRS GASCOIGNE: Th'art a fool.

MINNIE: And that's what you've done to me – that's my life spoiled – spoiled – ay, worse than if I'd had a drunken husband that knocked me about. For it's dead.

MRS GASCOIGNE: Tha'rt shoutin' because nowt ails thee – that's what tha art.

JOE: Nay, Mother, tha knows it's right. Tha knows tha's got me – an'll ha'e me till ter dies – an' after that – yi.

MRS GASCOIGNE: Tha talks like a fool.

JOE: And sometimes, Mother, I wish I wor dead, I do.

MINNIE: You see, you see! You see what you've done to them. It's strong women like you, who were too much for their husbands – ah!

JOE: Tha knows I couldna leave thee, Mother – tha knows I couldna. An' me, a young man, belongs to thy owd age. An' there's nowheer for me to go, Mother. For tha'rt gettin' nearer to death an' yet I canna leave thee to go my own road. An' I wish, yi, often, as I wor dead.

MRS GASCOIGNE: Dunna, lad – dunna let 'er put these ideas i' thy head.

JOE: An' I can but fritter my days away. There's no goin' forrard for me.

MRS GASCOIGNE: Nay, lad, nay – what lad's better off than thee, dost reckon?

JOE: If I went t'r Australia, th' best part on me wouldna go wi' me.

MRS GASCOIGNE: Tha wunna go t'r Australia!

JOE: If I went, I should be a husk of a man. I'm allers a husk of a man, Mother. There's nowt solid about me. The' isna.

MRS GASCOIGNE: Whativer dost mean? You've a' set on me at once.

JOE: I'm nowt, Mother, an' I count for nowt. Yi, an' I know it.

MRS GASCOIGNE: Tha does. Tha sounds as if tha counts for nowt, as a rule, doesn't ter?

JOE: There's not much of a man about me. T'other chaps is more of fools, but they more of men an' a' – an' they know it.

MRS GASCOIGNE: That's thy fault.

JOE: Yi – an' will be – ter th' end o' th' chapter.

[*Enter* LUTHER.]

MINNIE: Did you tell her?

LUTHER: Yes.

MINNIE: We'll have some tea, should we?

JOE: Ay, let's. For it's bin dry work.

[*She sets the kettle on.*]

MRS GASCOIGNE: I mun be goin'.

MINNIE: Wait and have a cup of tea. I brought a cake.

JOE: But we non goin' ter ha'e it, are we, Luther, these 'ere blacklegs goin' down interferin'.

LUTHER: We arena.

MRS GASCOIGNE: But how are you going to stop them?

JOE: We s'll manage it, one road or t'other.

MRS GASCOIGNE: You'll non go gettin' yourselves into trouble.

LUTHER: We in trouble enow.

MINNIE: If you'd have had Lizzie Charley in, what should you have paid her with?

LUTHER: We should ha' found the money somewhere.

MINNIE: Do you know what I had to keep house on this week, Mother?

MRS GASCOIGNE: Not much, sin' there wor nowt but ten shillin' strike pay.

MINNIE: He gave me five shillings.

LUTHER: Tha could ha' had what things ter wanted on strap.

MINNIE: No – but why should you keep, to drink on, as much as you give me to keep house on? Five shillings!

JOE: Five bob's non a whackin' sight o' pocket money for a man's week.

MINNIE: It is, if he earns nothing. It was that as finished me off.

JOE: Well, *tha* niver ned go short – tha can let *him*.

MINNIE: I knew that was what *he* thought. But if he wouldna have my money for one thing, he wasn't going to for another.

MRS GASCOIGNE: Why, what wouldn't he have it for?

MINNIE: He wouldn't have that forty pounds, when I went on my knees to beg and beseech him to.

LUTHER: Tha did! Tha throwed it at me as if I wor a beggar as stank.

MINNIE: And you wouldn't have it when I asked you.

LUTHER: No – an' wouldna ha'e it now.

MINNIE: You can't.

LUTHER: I dunna want it.

MINNIE: And if you don't find money to keep the house on, we shall both of us starve. For you've got to keep me. And I've got no money of my own now.

LUTHER: Why, what dost mean?

MINNIE: I mean what I say.

MRS GASCOIGNE: Why, what?

MINNIE: I was sick of having it between us. It was but a hundred and twenty. So I went to Manchester and spent it.

MRS GASCOIGNE: Tha's bin an' spent a hundred and twenty pound i' four days?

MINNIE: Yes, I have.

MRS GASCOIGNE: Whativer are we comin' to!

JOE: That wor a stroke worth two. Tell us what tha bought.

MINNIE: I bought myself a ring, for one thing. I thought if I ever had any children, and they asked me where was my engagement ring, I should have to show them something, for their father's sake. Do you like it? [*Holds out her hand to* JOE.]

JOE: My word, but that's a bobby-dazzler. Look, Mother.

MRS GASCOIGNE: H'm.

[JOE *takes the ring off.*]

JOE: My word, but that's a diamond, if you like. How much did it cost?

MINNIE: Thirty pounds. I've got the bill in my pocket.

MRS GASCOIGNE: I only hope you'll niver come to want some day.

MINNIE: Luther must see to that.

JOE: And what else did ter buy?

MINNIE: I'll show you. [*Gets her bag, unlocks it, takes out three prints.*]

JOE: I dunna reckon much ter these.

MRS GASCOIGNE: Nor me neither. An' how much has ter gen for them apiece?

MINNIE: That was twenty-five pounds. They're beautiful prints.

MRS GASCOIGNE: I dunna believe a word tha says.

MINNIE: I'll show you the bill. My master's a collector, and he picked them for me. He says they're well worth the money. And I like them.

MRS GASCOIGNE: Well, I niver seed such a job in my life. T-t-t-t! Well, a' I can say is, I hope tha'll niver come ter want. Throwin' good money i' th' gutter like this. Nay, I feel fair bad. Nay! T-t-t-t! Such tricks! And such bits o' dirty paper!

JOE: I'd rather ha'e the Co-op almanack.

MRS GASCOIGNE: So would I, any day! What dost say to't, our Luther?

LUTHER: 'Er does as 'er likes.

MINNIE: I had a lovely time with Mr Westlake, choosing them at the dealer's. He *is* clever.

MRS GASCOIGNE: Tha towd him tha wanted to get rid o' thy money, did ter?

MINNIE: No – I said I wanted some pictures for the parlour, and asked him if he'd help me choose.

MRS GASCOIGNE: Good money thrown away. Maybe the very bread of your children.

MINNIE: Nay, that's Luther's duty to provide.

MRS GASCOIGNE: Well, a' I can say is, I hope you may never come ter want. If our Luther died . . .

MINNIE: I should go back to work.

MRS GASCOIGNE: But what if tha'd three or four children?

MINNIE: A hundred and twenty pounds wouldn't make much odds then.

MRS GASCOIGNE: Well, a' I can say, I hope tha'lt niver live ter rue the day.

JOE: What dost think on 'er, Luther?

LUTHER: Nay, she's done as she liked with her own.

MINNIE [*emptying her purse in her lap*]: I've got just seventeen shillings. You drew your strike pay yesterday. How much have you got of that, Luther?

LUTHER: Three bob.

MINNIE: And do you want to keep it?

LUTHER: Ah.

MINNIE: Very well . . . I shall spend this seventeen shillings till it's gone, and then we shall have to live on soup-tickets.

MRS GASCOIGNE: I'll back my life!

JOE: And who'll fetch the soup?

MINNIE: Oh, I shall. I've been thinking, that big jug will do nicely. I'm in the same boat as other men's wives now, and so I must do the same.

JOE: They'll gi'e you strap at West's.

MINNIE: I'm not going to run up bills, no, I'm not. I'll go to the free teas, and fetch soup, an' with ten shillings a week we shall manage.

MRS GASCOIGNE: Well, that's one road, lass.

MINNIE: It's the only one. And now, if he can provide, he

must, and if he can't, he must tell me so, and I'll go back into service, and not be a burden to him.

MRS GASCOIGNE: High and mighty, high and mighty! We'll see, my lass; we'll see.

MINNIE: That's all we can do.

MRS GASCOIGNE: Tha doesna care how he takes it.

MINNIE: The prints belong to both of us. [*Hands them to* LUTHER.] You haven't said if you like them yet.

LUTHER [*taking them, suddenly rams them in the fire*]: Tha can go to hell.

MINNIE [*with a cry*]: Ah! – that's my ninety pounds gone. [*Tries to snatch them out.*]

MRS GASCOIGNE [*beginning to cry*]: Come, Joe, let's go; let's go, my lad. I've seen as much this day as ever my eyes want to see. Let's go, my lad. [*Gets up, beginning to tie on her bonnet.*]

MINNIE [*white and intense, to* LUTHER]: Should you like to throw my ring after them? It's all I've got left. [*She holds out her hand – he flings it from him.*]

LUTHER: Yi, what do I care what I do! [*Clenching his fists as if he would strike her.*] – what do I! – what do I – !

MRS GASCOIGNE [*putting on her shawl*]: A day's work – a day's work! Ninety pound! Nay – nay, oh, nay – nay, oh, nay – nay! Let's go, Joe, my lad. Eh, our Luther, our Luther! Let's go, Joe. Come.

JOE: Ah, I'll come, Mother.

MRS GASCOIGNE: Luther!

LUTHER: What?

MRS GASCOIGNE: It's a day's work, it is, wi' thee. Eh dear! Come, let's go, Joe. Let's go whoam.

LUTHER: An' I'll go.

MRS GASCOIGNE: Dunna thee do nowt as ter'll repent of, Luther – dunna thee. It's thy mother axes thee. Come, Joe.

[MRS GASCOIGNE *goes out, followed by* JOE. LUTHER *stands with face averted from his wife; mutters something, reaches for his cap, goes out.* MINNIE *stands with her hand on the mantelpiece.*]

CURTAIN

ACT FOUR

The following morning – about 5 a.m. A candle is burning.

MINNIE *sits by the fire in a dressing-gown. She is weeping. A knock, and* MRS GASCOIGNE'S *voice.* MINNIE *goes to open the door; re-enters with her mother-in-law, the latter with a big brown shawl over her head.*

MRS GASCOIGNE: Is Luther a-whoam?

MINNIE: No – he's not been in all night.

MRS GASCOIGNE: T-t-t-t! Now whereiver can they be? Joe's not in neither.

MINNIE: Isn't he?

MRS GASCOIGNE: No. He said he might be late, so I went to bed, and slept a bit uneasy-like till about four o'clock. Then I wakes up a' of a sudden, an' says: 'I'm by mysen i' th' house!' It gave me such a turn I daresn't shout. So I gets me up an' goes ter his room, an' he'd niver bin i' bed a' night. Well, I went down, but no signs nowhere. An' 'im wi' a broken arm. An' I listened an' I listened – an' then methinks I heered a gun go off. I felt as if I should die if I stopped by mysen another minute. So I on's wi' my shawl an' nips down here. There's not a soul astir nowhere. I a'most dropped when I seed your light. Hasn't Luther bin in a' night, dost say?

MINNIE: He went out with you, and he never came in again. I went to bed, thinking perhaps he'd be sleeping on the sofa. And then I came down, and he wasn't here.

MRS GASCOIGNE: Well, I've seen nowt of him, for he never come up to our house. – Now I wonder what's afoot wi' th' silly fools?

MINNIE: I thought he'd gone and left me.

MRS GASCOIGNE: It's more like some o' this strike work. When I heered that gun, I said: 'Theer goes one o' my lads!'

MINNIE: You don't think they're killed?

MRS GASCOIGNE: Heaven knows what they are. But I niver thought he'd ha' served me this trick – left me by mysen without telling me, and gone cutting off a' th' night through – an' him wi' a broken arm.

MINNIE: Where do you think they've gone?

MRS GASCOIGNE: The Lord above alone knows – but I'se warrant it's one o' these riotin' tricks – stopping them blacklegs as wor goin' down to see to th' roads.

MINNIE: Do you think – ?

MRS GASCOIGNE: I'll back anything. For I heered th' winding engines plain as anything. Hark!

[*They listen.*]

MINNIE: I believe I can hear them.

MRS GASCOIGNE: Th' ingines?

MINNIE: Yes.

MRS GASCOIGNE: They're winding something down. Eh dear, what a dead world it seems, wi' none o' th' pits chuffin' an' no steam wavin' by day, an' no lights shinin' by night. You may back your life there was a gang of 'em going to stop that lot of blacklegs. And there'd be soldiers for a certainty. If I didn't hear a shot, I heered summat much like one.

MINNIE: But they'd never shoot, would they?

MRS GASCOIGNE: Haven't they shot men up an' down th' country? Didn't I know them lads was pining to go an' be shot at? I did. Methinks when I heard that gun, 'They'd niver rest till this had happened.'

MINNIE: But they're not shot, Mother. You exaggerate.

MRS GASCOIGNE: I niver said they wor. But if anything happens to a man, my lass, you may back your life, nine cases out o' ten, it's a spit on th' women.

MINNIE: Oh, what a thing to say! Why, there are accidents.

MRS GASCOIGNE: Yes, an' men verily gets accidents, to pay us out, I do believe. They get huffed up, they bend down their faces, and they say to theirselves: 'Now I'll get myself hurt, an' she'll be sorry,' else: 'Now I'll get myself killed, an' she'll ha'e nobody to sleep wi' 'er, an' nobody to nag at.' Oh, my lass, I've had a husband an' six sons. Children they are, these men, but, my word, they're revengeful children. Children men is a' the days o' their lives. But they're master of us women when their dander's up, an' they pay us back double an' treble – they do – an' you mun allers expect it.

MINNIE: But if they went to stop the blacklegs, they wouldn't be doing it to spite us.

MRS GASCOIGNE: Wouldn't they! Yi, but they would. My lads 'ud do it to spite me, an' our Luther 'ud do it to spite thee. Yes – and it's trew. For they'd run theirselves into danger and lick their lips for joy, thinking, if I'm killed, then *she* maun lay me out. Yi – I seed it in our mester. He got killed a' pit. An' when I laid him out, his face wor that grim, an' his body that stiff, an' it said as plain as plain: 'Nowthen, you've done for me.' For it's risky work, handlin' men, my lass, an' niver thee pray for sons – Not but what daughters is any good. Th' world is made o' men, for me, lass – there's only the men for me. An' tha'rt similar. An' so, tha'lt reap trouble by the peck, an' sorrow by the bushel. For when a woman builds her life on men, either husbands or sons, she builds on summat as sooner or later brings the house down crash on her head – yi, she does.

MINNIE: But it depends how and what she builds.

MRS GASCOIGNE: It depends, it depends. An' tha thinks tha can steer clear o' what I've done. An' perhaps tha can. But steer clear the whole length o' th' road, tha canna, an' tha'lt see. Nay, a childt is a troublesome pleasure to a woman, but a man's a trouble pure and simple.

MINNIE: I'm sure it depends what you make of him.

MRS GASCOIGNE: Maybe – maybe. But I've allers tried to do my best, i' spite o' what tha said against me this afternoon.

MINNIE: I didn't mean it – I was in a rage.

MRS GASCOIGNE: Yi, tha meant it plain enow. But I've tried an' tried my best for my lads, I have – an' this is what owd age brings me – wi' 'em.

MINNIE: Nay, Mother – nay. See how fond they are of you.

MRS GASCOIGNE: Yi – an' they go now i' their mischief, yes, tryin' to get killed, to spite me. Yi!

MINNIE: Nay. Nay.

MRS GASCOIGNE: It's true. An' tha can ha'e Luther. Tha'lt get him, an' tha can ha'e him.

MINNIE: Do you think I shall?

MRS GASCOIGNE: I can see. Tha'lt get him – but tha'lt get sorrow wi' 'em, an' wi' th' sons tha has. See if tha doesna.

MINNIE: But I don't care. Only don't keep him from me. It leaves me so – with nothing – not even trouble.

MRS GASCOIGNE: He'll come to thee – an' he'll think no more o' me as is his mother than he will o' that poker.

MINNIE: Oh, no – oh, no.

MRS GASCOIGNE: Yi – I know well – an' then that other.

[*There is a silence – the two women listening.*]

MINNIE: If they'd been hurt, we should ha' known by now.

MRS GASCOIGNE: Happen we should. If they come, they'll come together. An' they'll come to this house first.

[*A silence.* MINNIE *starts.*]

Did ter hear owt?

MINNIE: Somebody got over the stile.

MRS GASCOIGNE [*listening*]: Yi.

MINNIE [*listening*]: It *is* somebody.

MRS GASCOIGNE: I' t'street.

MINNIE [*starting up*]: Yes.

MRS GASCOIGNE: Comin'? It's Luther. [*Goes to the door.*] An' it's on'y Luther.

[*Both women stand, the mother nearer the door. The door opens – a slight sluther. Enter* LUTHER, *with blood on his face – rather shaky and dishevelled.*]

My boy! my boy!

LUTHER: Mother! [*He goes blindly.*] Where's Minnie?

MINNIE [*with a cry*]: Oh!

MRS GASCOIGNE: Wheer's Joe? – wheer's our Joe?

LUTHER [*to* MINNIE, *queer, stunned, almost polite*]: It worn't 'cause I wor mad wi' thee I didna come whoam.

MRS GASCOIGNE [*clutching him sternly*]: Where's Joe?

LUTHER: He's gone up street – he thought tha might ha' wakkened.

MRS GASCOIGNE: Wakkened enow.

[MRS GASCOIGNE *goes out.*]

MINNIE: Oh, what have you done?

LUTHER: We'd promised not to tell nobody – else I should.

We stopped them blacklegs – leastways – but it worn't because I – I – [*He stops to think.*] I wor mad wi' thee, as I didna come whoam.

MINNIE: What have you done to your head?

LUTHER: It wor a stone or summat catched it. It's gev me a headache. Tha mun – tha mun tie a rag round it – if ter will. [*He sways as he takes his cap off.*]

[*She catches him in her arms. He leans on her as if he were tipsy.*] Minnie –

MINNIE: My love – my love!

LUTHER: Minnie – I want thee ter ma'e what tha can o' me. [*He sounds almost sleepy.*]

MINNIE [*crying*]: My love – my love!

LUTHER: I know what tha says is true.

MINNIE: No, my love – it isn't – it isn't.

LUTHER: But if ter'lt ma'e what ter can o' me – an' then if ter has a childt – tha'lt happen ha'e enow.

MINNIE: No – no – it's you. It's you I want. It's you.

LUTHER: But tha's allers had me.

MINNIE: No, never – and it hurt so.

LUTHER: I thowt tha despised me.

MINNIE: Ah – my love!

LUTHER: Dunna say I'm mean, to me – an' got no go.

MINNIE: I only said it because you wouldn't let me love you.

LUTHER: Tha didna love me.

MINNIE: Ha! – it was *you*.

LUTHER: Yi. [*He looses himself and sits down heavily.*] I'll ta'e my boots off. [*He bends forward.*]

MINNIE: Let me do them. [*He sits up again.*]

LUTHER: It's started bleedin'. I'll do 'em i' ha'ef a minute.

MINNIE: No – trust me – trust yourself to me. Let me have you now for my own. [*She begins to undo his boots.*]

LUTHER: Dost want me?

MINNIE [*she kisses his hands*]: Oh, my love! [*She takes him in her arms.*]

[*He suddenly begins to cry.*]

CURTAIN

THE WIDOWING OF
MRS HOLROYD

A PLAY IN THREE ACTS
(1914)

CHARACTERS

MRS HOLROYD
HOLROYD
BLACKMORE
JACK HOLROYD
MINNIE HOLROYD
GRANDMOTHER
RIGLEY
CLARA
LAURA
MANAGER
TWO MINERS

The action of the play takes place in the Holroyds' cottage.

ACT ONE

SCENE I

The kitchen of a miner's small cottage. On the left is the fireplace, with a deep, full red fire. At the back is a white-curtained window, and beside it the outer door of the room. On the right, two white wooden stairs intrude into the kitchen below the closed stair-foot door. On the left, another door.

The room is furnished with a chintz-backed sofa under the window, a glass-knobbed painted dresser on the right, and in the centre, toward the fire, a table with a red and blue check tablecloth. On one side of the hearth is a wooden rocking-chair, on the other an arm-chair of round staves. An unlighted copper-shaded lamp hangs from the raftered ceiling. It is dark twilight, with the room full of warm fireglow. A woman enters from the outer door. As she leaves the door open behind her, the colliery rail can be seen not far from the threshold, and, away back, the headstocks of a pit.

The woman is tall and voluptuously built. She carries a basket heaped full of washing, which she has just taken from the clotheslines outside. Setting down the basket heavily, she feels among the clothes. She lifts out a white heap of sheets and other linen, setting it on the table; then she takes a woollen shirt in her hand.

MRS HOLROYD [*aloud, to herself*]: You know they're not dry even now, though it's been as fine as it has. [*She spreads the shirt on the back of her rocking-chair, which she turns to the fire.*]

VOICE [*calling from outside*]: Well, have you got them dry?

[MRS HOLROYD *starts up, turns and flings her hand in the direction of the open door, where appears a man in blue overalls, swarfed and greased. He carries a dinner-basket.*]

MRS HOLROYD: You – you – I don't know what to call you! The idea of shouting at me like that – like the Evil One out of the darkness!

BLACKMORE: I ought to have remembered your tender nerves. Shall I come in?

MRS HOLROYD: No – not for your impudence. But you're late, aren't you?

BLACKMORE: It's only just gone six. We electricians, you know, we're the gentlemen on a mine: ours is gentlemen's work. But I'll bet Charles Holroyd was home before four.

MRS HOLROYD [*bitterly*]: Ay, and gone again before five.

BLACKMORE: But mine's a lad's job, and I do nothing! – Where's he gone?

MRS HOLROYD [*contemptuously*]: Dunno! He'd got a game on somewhere – toffed himself up to the nines, and skedaddled off as brisk as a turkey-cock. [*She smirks in front of the mirror hanging on the chimney-piece, in imitation of a man brushing his hair and moustache and admiring himself.*]

BLACKMORE: Though turkey-cocks aren't brisk as a rule. Children playing?

MRS HOLROYD [*recovering herself, coldly*]: Yes. And they ought to be in. [*She continues placing the flannel garments before the fire, on the fender and on chair-backs, till the stove is hedged in with a steaming fence; then she takes a sheet in a bundle from the table, and goes up to* BLACKMORE, *who stands watching her.*] Here, take hold, and help me fold it.

BLACKMORE: I shall swarf it up.

MRS HOLROYD [*snatching back the sheet*]: Oh, you're as tiresome as everybody else.

BLACKMORE [*putting down his basket and moving to door on right*]: Well, I can soon wash my hands.

MRS HOLROYD [*ceasing to flap and fold pillow-cases*]: That roller-towel's ever so dirty. I'll get you another. [*She goes to a drawer in the dresser, and then back toward the scullery, from which comes the sound of water.*]

BLACKMORE: Why, bless my life, I'm a lot dirtier than the towel. I don't want another.

MRS HOLROYD [*going into the scullery*]: Here you are.

BLACKMORE [*softly, now she is near him*]: Why did you trouble now? Pride, you know, pride, nothing else.

MRS HOLROYD [*also playful*]: It's nothing but decency.

BLACKMORE [*softly*]: Pride, pride, pride!

[*A child of eight suddenly appears in the doorway.*]

JACK: Oo, how dark!

MRS HOLROYD [*hurrying agitated into the kitchen*]: Why, where have you been – what have you been doing now?

JACK [*surprised*]: Why – I've only been out to play.

MRS HOLROYD [*still sharply*]: And where's Minnie?
[*A little girl of six appears by the door.*]

MINNIE: I'm here, mam, and what do you think – ?

MRS HOLROYD [*softening, as she recovers equanimity*]: Well, and what should I think?

JACK: Oh, yes, mam – you know my father – ?

MRS HOLROYD [*ironically*]: I should hope so.

MINNIE: We saw him dancing, mam, with a paper bonnet.

MRS HOLROYD: What – ?

JACK: There's some women at New Inn, what's come from Nottingham –

MINNIE: An' he's dancin' with the pink one.

JACK: Shut up, our Minnie. An' they've got paper bonnets on –

MINNIE: All colours, mam!

JACK [*getting angry*]: Shut up, our Minnie! An' my dad's dancing with her.

MINNIE: With the pink-bonnet one, mam.

JACK: Up in the club-room over the bar.

MINNIE: An' she's a lot littler than him, mam.

JACK [*piteously*]: Shut up, our Minnie – An' you can see 'em go past the window, 'cause there isn't no curtains up, an' my father's got the pink-bonnet one –

MINNIE: An' there's a piano, mam –

JACK: An' lots of folks outside watchin', lookin' at my dad! He can dance, can't he, mam?

MRS HOLROYD [*she has been lighting the lamp, and holds the lamp-glass*]: And who else is there?

MINNIE: Some more men – an' *all* the women with paper bonnets on.

JACK: There's about ten, I should think, an' they say they came in a brake from Nottingham.

[MRS HOLROYD, *trying to replace the lamp-glass over the flame, lets it drop on the floor with a smash.*]

JACK: There, now – now we'll have to have a candle.

BLACKMORE [*appearing in the scullery doorway with the towel*]: What's that – the lamp-glass?

JACK: I never knowed Mr Blackmore was here.

BLACKMORE [*to* MRS HOLROYD]: Have you got another?

MRS HOLROYD: No. [*There is silence for a moment.*] We can manage with a candle for to-night.

BLACKMORE [*stepping forward and blowing out the smoky flame*]: I'll see if I can't get you one from the pit. I shan't be a minute.

MRS HOLROYD: Don't – don't bother – I don't want you to. [*He, however, unscrews the burner and goes.*]

MINNIE: Did Mr Blackmore come for tea, mam?

MRS HOLROYD: No; he's had no tea.

JACK: I bet he's hungry. Can I have some bread?

MRS HOLROYD [*she stands a lighted candle on the table*]: Yes, and you can get your boots off to go to bed.

JACK: It's not seven o'clock yet.

MRS HOLROYD: It doesn't matter.

MINNIE: What do they wear paper bonnets for, mam?

MRS HOLROYD: Because they're brazen hussies.

JACK: I saw them having a glass of beer.

MRS HOLROYD: A nice crew!

JACK: They say they are old pals of Mrs Meakins. You could hear her screaming o' laughin', an' my dad says: 'He-ah, missis – here – a dog's nose for the Dachess – hopin' it'll smell samthing' – What's a dog's-nose?

MRS HOLROYD [*giving him a piece of bread and butter*]: Don't ask me, child. How should I know?

MINNIE: Would she eat it, mam?

MRS HOLROYD: Eat what?

MINNIE: Her in the pink bonnet – eat the dog's-nose?

MRS HOLROYD: No, of course not. How should I know what a dog's-nose is?

JACK: I bet he'll never go to work to-morrow, mother – will he?

MRS HOLROYD: Goodness knows. I'm sick of it – disgracing me. There'll be the whole place cackling *this* now. They've no sooner finished about him getting taken up for fighting than they begin on this. But I'll put a stop to it some road or other. It's not going on, if I know it: it isn't. [*She stops, hearing footsteps, and* BLACKMORE *enters.*]

BLACKMORE: Here we are then – got one all right.

MINNIE: Did they give it you, Mr Blackmore?

BLACKMORE: No, I took it. [*He screws on the burner and proceeds to light the lamp. He is a tall, slender, mobile man of twenty-seven, brown-haired, dressed in blue overalls.* JACK HOLROYD *is a big, dark, ruddy, lusty lad.* MINNIE *is also big, but fair.*]

MINNIE: What do you wear blue trousers for, Mr Blackmore?

BLACKMORE: They're to keep my other trousers from getting greasy.

MINNIE: Why don't you wear pit-breeches, like dad's?

JACK: 'Cause he's a 'lectrician. Could you make me a little injun what would make electric light?

BLACKMORE: I will, some day.

JACK: When?

MINNIE: Why don't you come an' live here?

BLACKMORE [*looking swiftly at* MRS HOLROYD]: Nay, you've got your own dad to live here.

MINNIE [*plaintively*]: Well, you could come as well. Dad shouts when we've gone to bed, an' thumps the table. He wouldn't if you was here.

JACK: He dursn't –

MRS HOLROYD: Be quiet now, be quiet. Here, Mr Blackmore. [*She again gives him the sheet to fold.*]

BLACKMORE: Your hands *are* cold.

MRS HOLROYD: Are they? – I didn't know.
   [BLACKMORE *puts his hand on hers.*]

MRS HOLROYD [*confusedly, looking aside*]: You must want your tea.

BLACKMORE: I'm in no hurry.

MRS HOLROYD: Selvidge to selvidge. You'll be quite a domestic man, if you go on.

BLACKMORE: Ay.
   [*They fold the two sheets.*]

BLACKMORE: They are white, your sheets!

MRS HOLROYD: But look at the smuts on them – look! This vile hole! I'd never have come to live here, in all the thick of the pit-grime, and lonely, if it hadn't been for him, so that he shouldn't call in a public-house on his road home from work. And now he slinks past on the other side of the railway, and goes down to the New Inn instead of coming in for his dinner. I might as well have stopped in Bestwood.

BLACKMORE: Though I rather like this little place, standing by itself.

MRS HOLROYD: Jack, can you go and take the stockings in for me? They're on the line just below the pigsty. The prop's near the apple-tree – mind it. Minnie, you take the peg-basket.

MINNIE: Will there be any rats, mam?

MRS HOLROYD: Rats – no. They'll be frightened when they hear you, if there are.

[*The children go out.*]

BLACKMORE: Poor little beggars!

MRS HOLROYD: Do you know, this place is fairly alive with rats. They run up that dirty vine in front of the house – I'm always at him to cut it down – and you can hear them at night overhead like a regiment of soldiers tramping. Really, you know, I *hate* them.

BLACKMORE: Well – a rat is a nasty thing!

MRS HOLROYD: But I s'll get used to them. I'd give anything to be out of this place.

BLACKMORE: It *is* rotten, when you're tied to a life you don't like. But I should miss it if you weren't here. When I'm coming down the line to the pit in the morning – it's nearly dark at seven now – I watch the firelight in here. Sometimes I put my hand on the wall outside where the chimney runs up to feel it warm. There isn't much in Bestwood, is there?

MRS HOLROYD: There's less than nothing if you can't be like the rest of them – as common as they're made.

BLACKMORE: It's a fact – particularly for a woman – But this place is cosy – God love me, I'm sick of lodgings.

MRS HOLROYD: You'll have to get married – I'm sure there are plenty of nice girls about.

BLACKMORE: Are there? I never see 'em. [*He laughs.*]

MRS HOLROYD: Oh, come, you can't say that.

BLACKMORE: I've not seen a single girl – an unmarried girl that I should want for more than a fortnight – not one.

MRS HOLROYD: Perhaps you're very particular. [*She puts her two palms on the table and leans back. He draws near to her, dropping his head.*]

BLACKMORE: Look here! [*He has put his hand on the table near hers.*]

MRS HOLROYD: Yes, I know you've got nice hands – but you needn't be vain of them.

BLACKMORE: No – it's not that – But don't they seem – [*he glances swiftly at her; she turns her head aside; he laughs nervously*] – they sort of go well with one another. [*He laughs again.*]

MRS HOLROYD: They *do*, rather –
[*They stand still, near one another, with bent heads, for a moment. Suddenly she starts up and draws her hand away.*]

BLACKMORE: Why – what is it?
[*She does not answer. The children come in –* JACK *with an armful of stockings,* MINNIE *with the basket of pegs.*]

JACK: I believe it's freezing, mother.

MINNIE: Mr Blackmore, could you shoot a rat an' hit it?

BLACKMORE [*laughing*]: Shoot the lot of 'em, like a wink.

MRS HOLROYD: But you've had no tea. What an awful shame to keep you here!

BLACKMORE: Nay, I don't care. It never bothers me.

MRS HOLROYD: Then you're different from most men.

BLACKMORE: All men aren't alike, you know.

MRS HOLROYD: But do go and get some tea.

MINNIE [*plaintively*]: Can't you stop, Mr Blackmore?

BLACKMORE: Why Minnie?

MINNIE: So's we're not frightened. Yes, do. Will you?

BLACKMORE: Frightened of what?

MINNIE: 'Cause there's noises, an' rats – an' perhaps dad'll come home and shout.

BLACKMORE: But he'd shout more if I was here.

JACK: He doesn't when my uncle John's here. So you stop, an' perhaps he won't.

BLACKMORE: Don't you like him to shout when you're in bed?

[*They do not answer, but look seriously at him.*]

CURTAIN

SCENE II

The same scene, two hours later. The clothes are folded in little piles on the table and the sofa. MRS HOLROYD *is folding a thick flannel undervest or singlet which her husband wears in the pit and which has just dried on the fender.*

MRS HOLROYD [*to herself*]: Now, thank goodness, they're all dried. It's only nine o'clock, so he won't be in for another two hours, the nuisance. [*She sits on the sofa, letting her arms hang down in dejection. After a minute or two she jumps up, to begin rudely dropping the piles of washed clothes in the basket.*] I don't care, I'm not going to let him have it all *his* way – no! [*She weeps a little, fiercely, drying her eyes on the edge of her white apron.*] Why should *I* put up with it all? – He can do what he likes. But I don't care, no, I don't – [*She flings down the full clothes-basket, sits suddenly in the rocking-chair, and weeps. There is the sound of coarse, bursting laughter, in vain subdued, and a man's deep guffaws. Footsteps draw near. Suddenly the door opens, and a little, plump, pretty woman of thirty, in a close-fitting dress and a giddy, frilled bonnet of pink paper, stands perkily in the doorway.* MRS HOLROYD *springs up; her small, sensitive nose is inflamed with weeping, her eyes are wet and flashing. She fronts the other woman.*]

CLARA [*with a pert smile and a jerk of the head*]: Good evenin'!

MRS HOLROYD: What do you want?

CLARA [*she has a Yorkshire accent*]: Oh, we've not come beggin' – this is a visit. [*She stuffs her handkerchief in front of her mouth in a little snorting burst of laughter. There is the sound of another woman behind going off into uncontrollable laughter, while a man guffaws.*]

MRS HOLROYD [*after a moment of impotence – tragically*]: What – !

CLARA [*faltering slightly, affecting a polite tone*]: We thought we'd just call – [*She stuffs her handkerchief in front of her explosive laughter – the other woman shrieks again, beginning high, and running down the scale.*]

MRS HOLROYD: What do you mean? – What do you want here?

CLARA [*she bites her lip*]: We don't want anything, thanks. We've just called. [*She begins to laugh again – so does the other.*] Well, I don't think much of the manners in this part of the country. [*She takes a few hesitating steps into the kitchen.*]

MRS HOLROYD [*trying to shut the door upon her*]: No, you are not coming in.

CLARA [*preventing her closing the door*]: Dear me, what a to-do! [*She struggles with the door. The other woman comes up to help; a man is seen in the background.*]

LAURA: My word, aren't we good enough to come in?
[MRS HOLROYD, *finding herself confronted by what seems to her excitement a crowd, releases the door and draws back a little – almost in tears of anger.*]

MRS HOLROYD: You have no business here. What do you want?

CLARA [*putting her bonnet straight and entering in brisk defiance*]: I tell you we've only come to see you. [*She looks round the kitchen, then makes a gesture toward the arm-chair.*] Can I sit here? [*She plumps herself down.*] Rest for the weary.
[*A woman and a man have followed her into the room.* LAURA *is highly coloured, stout, some forty years old, wears a blue paper bonnet, and looks like the landlady of a public-house. Both she and* CLARA *wear much jewellery.* LAURA *is well dressed in a blue cloth dress.* HOLROYD *is a big blond man. His cap is pushed back, and he looks rather tipsy and lawless. He has a heavy blond moustache. His jacket and trousers are black, his vest grey, and he wears a turn-down collar with dark bow.*]

LAURA [*sitting down in a chair on right, her hand on her bosom, panting*]: I've laughed till I feel fair bad.

CLARA: 'Aven't you got a drop of nothink to offer us, mester? Come, you are slow. I should 'ave thought a gentleman like you would have been out with the glasses afore we could have got breaths to ask you.

HOLROYD [*clumsily*]: I dunna believe there's owt in th' 'ouse but a bottle of stout.

CLARA [*putting her hand on her stomach*]: It feels as if th' kettle's going to boil over. [*She stuffs her handkerchief in front of her mouth, throws back her head, and snorts with laughter, having now regained her confidence.* LAURA *laughs in the last state of exhaustion, her hand on her breast.*]

HOLROYD: Shall ta ha'e it then?

CLARA: What do you say, Laura – are you having a drop?

LAURA [*submissively, and naturally tongue-tied*]: Well – I don't mind – I will if *you* do.

CLARA [*recklessly*]: I think we'll 'ave a drop, Charlie, an' risk it. It'll 'appen hold the rest down.

[*There is a moment of silence, while* HOLROYD *goes into the scullery.* CLARA *surveys the room and the dramatic pose of* MRS HOLROYD *curiously.*]

HOLROYD [*suddenly*]: Heh! What, come 'ere – !

[*There is a smash of pots, and a rat careers out of the scullery.* LAURA, *the first to see it, utters a scream, but is fastened to her chair, unable to move.*]

CLARA [*jumps up to the table, crying*]: It's a rat – Oh, save us! [*She scrambles up, banging her head on the lamp, which swings violently.*]

MRS HOLROYD [*who, with a little shriek, jerks her legs up on to the sofa, where she was stiffly reclining, now cries in despairing falsetto, stretching forth her arms*]: The lamp – mind, the lamp!

[CLARA *steadies the lamp, and holds her hand to her head.*]

HOLROYD [*coming from the scullery, a bottle of stout in his hand*]: Where is he?

CLARA: I believe he's gone under the sofa. My, an' he's a thumper, if you like, as big as a rabbit.

[HOLROYD *advances cautiously toward the sofa.*]

LAURA [*springing suddenly into life*]: Hi, hi, let me go – let me go – Don't touch him – Where is he? [*She flees and scrambles on to* CLARA'S *arm-chair, catching hold of the latter's skirts.*]

CLARA: Hang off – do you want to have a body down – Mind, I tell you.

MRS HOLROYD [*bunched up on the sofa, with crossed hands holding her arms, fascinated, watches her husband as he approaches to stoop and attack the rat; she suddenly screams*]: Don't, he'll fly at you.

HOLROYD: He'll not get a chance.

MRS HOLROYD: He will, he will – and they're poisonous! [*She ends on a very high note. Leaning forward on the sofa as far as she dares, she stretches out her arms to keep back her husband, who is about to kneel and search under the sofa for the rat.*]

HOLROYD: Come off, I canna see him.

MRS HOLROYD: I won't let you; he'll fly at you.

HOLROYD: I'll settle him –

MRS HOLROYD: Open the door and let him go.

HOLROYD: I shonna. I'll settle him. Shut thy claver. He'll non come anigh thee. [*He kneels down and begins to creep to the sofa. With a great bound,* MRS HOLROYD *flies to the door and flings it open. Then she rushes back to the couch.*]

CLARA: There he goes!

HOLROYD [*simultaneously*]: Hi! – Usszsa! [*He flings the bottle of stout out of the door.*]

LAURA [*piteously*]: Shut the door, do.

> [HOLROYD *rises, dusting his trousers knees, and closes the door.* LAURA *heavily descends and drops in the chair.*]

CLARA: Here, come an' help us down, Charlie. Look at her; she's going off.

> [*Though* LAURA *is still purple-red, she sinks back in the chair.* HOLROYD *goes to the table.* CLARA *places her hands on his shoulders and jumps lightly down. Then she pushes* HOLROYD *with her elbow.*]

Look sharp, get a glass of water. [*She unfastens* LAURA'S *collar and pulls off the paper bonnet.* MRS HOLROYD *sits up, straightens her clothing, and tries to look cold and contemptuous.* HOLROYD *brings a cup of water.* CLARA *sprinkles her friend's face.* LAURA *sighs and sighs again very deeply, then draws herself up painfully.*]

CLARA [*tenderly*]: Do you feel any better – shall you have a drink of water?

[LAURA *mournfully shakes her head;* CLARA *turns sharply to* HOLROYD.]

She'll 'ave a drop o' something.

[HOLROYD *goes out.* CLARA *meanwhile fans her friend with a handkerchief.* HOLROYD *brings stout. She pours out the stout, smells the glass, smells the bottle – then finally the cork.*]

Eh, mester, it's all of a work – it's had a foisty cork.

[*At that instant the stairfoot door opens slowly, revealing the children – the girl peering over the boy's shoulder – both in white nightgowns. Everybody starts.* LAURA *gives a little cry, presses her hand on her bosom, and sinks back, gasping.*]

CLARA [*appealing and anxious, to* MRS HOLROYD]: You don't 'appen to 'ave a drop of brandy for her, do you, missis?

[MRS HOLROYD *rises coldly without replying, and goes to the stairfoot door where the children stand.*]

MRS HOLROYD [*sternly, to the children*]: Go to bed!

JACK: What's a matter, mother?

MRS HOLROYD: Never you mind, go to bed!

CLARA [*appealingly*]: Be quick, missis.

[MRS HOLROYD, *glancing round, sees* LAURA *going purple, and runs past the children upstairs. The boy and girl sit on the lowest stair. Their father goes out of the house, shamefaced.* MRS HOLROYD *runs downstairs with a little brandy in a large bottle.*]

CLARA: Thanks, awfully. [*To* LAURA] Come on, try an' drink a drop, there's a dear.

[*They administer brandy to* LAURA. *The children sit watching, open-eyed. The girl stands up to look.*]

MINNIE [*whispering*]: I believe it's blue bonnet.

JACK [*whispering*]: It isn't – she's in a fit.

MINNIE [*whispering*]: Well, look under th' table – [JACK *peers under*] – there's 'er bonnet. [JACK *creeps forward.*] Come back, our Jack.

JACK [*returns with the bonnet*]: It's all made of paper.

MINNIE: Let's have a look – it's stuck together, not sewed.
[*She tries it on.* HOLROYD *enters – he looks at the child.*]

MRS HOLROYD [*sharply, glancing round*]: Take that off!
[MINNIE *hurriedly takes the bonnet from her head. Her father snatches it from her and puts it on the fire.*]

CLARA: There, you're coming round now, love.
[MRS HOLROYD *turns away. She sees* HOLROYD'S *eyes on the brandy-bottle, and immediately removes it, corking it up.*]

MRS HOLROYD [*to* CLARA]: You will not need this any more?

CLARA: No, thanks. I'm very much obliged.

MRS HOLROYD [*does not unbend, but speaks coldly to the children*]:
Come, this is no place for you – come back to bed.

MINNIE: No, mam, I don't want to.

MRS HOLROYD [*contralto*]: Come along!

MINNIE: I'm frightened, mam.

MRS HOLROYD: Frightened, what of?

MINNIE: Oo, there *was* a row.

MRS HOLROYD [*taking* MINNIE *in her arms*]: Did they frighten
you, my pet? [*She kisses her.*]

JACK [*in a high whisper*]: Mother, it's pink bonnet and blue
bonnet, what was dancing.

MINNIE [*whimpering*]: I don't want to go to bed, mam, I'm
frightened.

CLARA [*who has pulled off her pink bonnet and revealed a jug-
handle coiffure*]: We're going now, duckie – you're not
frightened of us, are you?
[MRS HOLROYD *takes the girl away before she can answer.*
JACK *lingers behind.*]

HOLROYD: Now then, get off after your mother.

JACK [*taking no notice of his father*]: I say, what's a dog's-nose?
[CLARA *ups with her handkerchief and* LAURA *responds with
a faint giggle.*]

HOLROYD: Go thy ways upstairs.

CLARA: It's only a small whiskey with a spoonful of beer in
it, my duck.

JACK: Oh!

CLARA: Come here, my duck, come on.
[JACK, *curious, advances.*]

CLARA: You'll tell your mother we didn't mean no harm, won't you?

JACK [*touching her earrings*]: What are they made of?

CLARA: They're only earrings. Don't you like them?

JACK: Um! [*He stands surveying her curiously. Then he touches a bracelet made of many little mosaic brooches.*] This is pretty, isn't it?

CLARA [*pleased*]: Do you like it? [*She takes it off. Suddenly* MRS HOLROYD *is heard calling, 'Jack, Jack!'* CLARA *starts.*]

HOLROYD: Now then, get off!

CLARA [*as* JACK *is reluctantly going*]: Kiss me good night, duckie, an' give this to your sister, shall you? [*She hands* JACK *the mosaic bracelet. He takes it doubtfully. She kisses him.* HOLROYD *watches in silence.*]

LAURA [*suddenly, pathetically*]: Aren't you going to give me a kiss, an' all?

[JACK *yields her his cheek, then goes.*]

CLARA [*to* HOLROYD]: Aren't they nice children?

HOLROYD: Ay.

CLARA [*briskly*]: Oh, dear, you're very short, all of a sudden. Don't answer if it hurts you.

LAURA: My, isn't he different?

HOLROYD [*laughing forcedly*]: I'm no different.

CLARA: Yes, you are. You shouldn't 'ave brought us if you was going to turn funny over it.

HOLROYD: I'm not funny.

CLARA: No, you're not. [*She begins to laugh.* LAURA *joins in in spite of herself.*] You're about as solemn as a roast potato. [*She flings up her hands, claps them down on her knees, and sways up and down as she laughs,* LAURA *joining in, hand on breast.*] Are you ready to be mashed? [*She goes off again – then suddenly wipes the laughter off her mouth and is solemn.*] But look 'ere, this'll never do. Now I'm going to be quiet. [*She prims herself.*]

HOLROYD: Tha'd 'appen better.

CLARA: Oh, indeed! You think I've got to pull a mug to look decent? You'd have to pull a big un, at that rate. [*She bubbles off, uncontrollably – shaking herself in exasperation meanwhile.* LAURA *joins in.* HOLROYD *leans over close to her.*]

HOLROYD: Tha's got plenty o' fizz in thee, seemly.

CLARA [*putting her hand on his face and pushing it aside, but leaving her hand over his cheek and mouth like a caress*]: Don't, you've been drinking. [*She begins to laugh.*]

HOLROYD: Should we be goin' then?

CLARA: Where do you want to take us?

HOLROYD: Oh – you please yourself o' that! Come on wi' me.

CLARA [*sitting up prim*]: Oh, indeed!

HOLROYD [*catching hold of her*]: Come on, let's be movin' – [*he glances apprehensively at the stairs*].

CLARA: What's your hurry?

HOLROYD [*persuasively*]: Yi, come on wi' thee.

CLARA: I don't think. [*She goes off, uncontrollably.*]

HOLROYD [*sitting on the table, just above her*]: What's use o' sittin' 'ere?

CLARA: I'm very comfy: I thank thee.

HOLROYD: Tha't a baffling little 'ussy.

CLARA [*running her hand along his thigh*]: Aren't you havin' nothing, my dear? [*Offers him her glass.*]

HOLROYD [*getting down from the table and putting his hand forcibly on her shoulder*]: No. Come on, let's shift.

CLARA [*struggling*]: Hands off! [*She fetches him a sharp slap across the face.* MRS HOLROYD *is heard coming downstairs.* CLARA, *released, sits down, smoothing herself.* HOLROYD *looks evil. He goes out to the door.*]

CLARA [*to* MRS HOLROYD, *penitently*]: I don't know what you think of us, I'm sure.

MRS HOLROYD: I think nothing at all.

CLARA [*bubbling*]: So you fix your thoughts elsewhere, do you? [*Suddenly changing to seriousness.*] No, but I *have* been awful to-night.

MRS HOLROYD [*contralto, emphatic*]: I don't want to know anything about you. I shall be glad when you'll go.

CLARA: Turning-out time, Laura.

LAURA [*turtling*]: I'm sorry, I'm sure.

CLARA: Never mind. But as true as I'm here, missis, I should never ha' come if I'd thought. But I had a drop – it all started with your husband sayin' he wasn't a married man.

LAURA [*laughing and wiping her eyes*]: I've never knowed her to go off like it – it's after the time she's had.

CLARA: You know, my husband was a brute to me – an' I was in bed three month after he died. He was a brute, he was. This is the first time I've been out; it's a'most the first laugh I've had for a year.

LAURA: It's true, what she says. We thought she'd go out of 'er mind. She never spoke a word for a fortnight.

CLARA: Though he's only been dead for two months, he was a brute to me. I was as nice a young girl as you could wish when I married him and went to the Fleece Inn – I was.

LAURA: Killed hisself drinking. An' she's that excitable, she is. We s'll 'ave an awful time with 'er to-morrow, I know.

MRS HOLROYD [*coldly*]: I don't know why I should hear all this.

CLARA: I know. I must 'ave seemed awful. An' them children – aren't they nice little things, Laura?

LAURA: They are that.

HOLROYD [*entering from the door*]: Hanna you about done theer?

CLARA: My word, if this is the way you treat a lady when she comes to see you. [*She rises.*]

HOLROYD: I'll see you down th' line.

CLARA: You're not coming a stride with us.

LAURA: We've got no hat, neither of us.

CLARA: We've got our own hair on our heads, at any rate. [*Drawing herself up suddenly in front of* MRS HOLROYD.] An' I've been educated at a boarding school as good as anybody. I can behave myself either in the drawing-room or in the kitchen as is fitting and proper. But if you'd buried a husband like mine, you wouldn't feel you'd much left to be proud of – an' you might go off occasionally.

MRS HOLROYD: I don't want to hear you.

CLARA [*bobbing a curtsy*]: Sorry I spoke. [*She goes out stiffly, followed by* LAURA.]

HOLROYD [*going forward*]: You mun mind th' points down th' line.

CLARA'S VOICE: I thank thee, Charlie – mind thy own points.
[*He hesitates at the door – returns and sits down. There is silence in the room.* HOLROYD *sits with his chin in his hand.* MRS HOLROYD *listens. The footsteps and voices of the two women die out. Then she closes the door.* HOLROYD *begins to unlace his boots.*]

HOLROYD [*ashamed yet defiant, withal anxious to apologize*]: Wheer's my slippers?
[MRS HOLROYD *sits on the sofa with face averted and does not answer.*]

HOLROYD: Dost hear? [*He pulls off his boots, noisily, and begins to hunt under the sofa.*] I canna find the things. [*No answer.*] Humph! – then I'll do be 'out 'em. [*He stumps about in his stockinged feet; going into the scullery, he brings out the loaf of bread; he returns into the scullery.*] Wheer's th' cheese? [*No answer – suddenly*] God blast it! [*He hobbles into the kitchen.*] I've trod on that broken basin, an' cut my foot open.
[MRS HOLROYD *refuses to take any notice. He sits down and looks at his sole – pulls off his stocking and looks again.*]
It's lamed me for life.
[MRS HOLROYD *glances at the wound.*]
Are na' ter goin' ter get me öwt for it?

MRS HOLROYD: Psh!

HOLROYD: Oh, a' right then. [*He hops to the dresser, opens a drawer, and pulls out a white rag; he is about to tear it.*]

MRS HOLROYD [*snatching it from him*]: Don't tear that!

HOLROYD [*shouting*]: Then what the deuce am I to do?
[MRS HOLROYD *sits stonily.*]
Oh, a' right then! [*He hops back to his chair, sits down, and begins to pull on his stocking.*] A' right then – a' right then. [*In a fever of rage he begins pulling on his boots.*] I'll go where I *can* find a bit o' rag.

MRS HOLROYD: Yes, that's what you want! All you want is an excuse to be off again – 'a bit of rag'!

HOLROYD [*shouting*]: An' what man'd want to stop in wi' a woman sittin' as fow as a jackass, an' canna get a word from 'er edgeways.

MRS HOLROYD: Don't expect me to speak to you after to-night's show. How dare you bring them to my house, how dare you?

HOLROYD: They've non hurt your house, have they?

MRS HOLROYD: I wonder you dare to cross the doorstep.

HOLROYD: I s'll do what the deuce I like. They're as good as you are.

MRS HOLROYD [*stands speechless, staring at him; then low*]: Don't you come near me again –

HOLROYD [*suddenly shouting, to get his courage up*]: She's as good as you are, every bit of it.

MRS HOLROYD [*blazing*]: Whatever I was and whatever I may be, don't you ever come near me again.

HOLROYD: What! I'll show thee. What's the hurt to you if a woman comes to the house? They're women as good as yourself, every whit of it.

MRS HOLROYD: Say no more. *Go* with them then, and don't come back.

HOLROYD: What! Yi, I will go, an' you s'll see. What! You think you're something, since your uncle left you that money, an' Blackymore puttin' you up to it. I can see your little game. I'm not as daft as you imagine. I'm no fool, I tell you.

MRS HOLROYD: No, you're not. You're a drunken beast, that's all you are.

HOLROYD: What, what – I'm what? I'll show you who's gaffer, though. [*He threatens her.*]

MRS HOLROYD [*between her teeth*]: No, it's not going on. If *you* won't go, I will.

HOLROYD: Go then, for you've always been too big for your shoes, in my house –

MRS HOLROYD: Yes – I ought never to have looked at you. Only you showed a fair face then.

HOLROYD: What! What! We'll see who's master i' this house. I tell you, I'm goin' to put a stop to it. [*He brings his fist down on the table with a bang.*] It's going to stop. [*He bangs the table again.*] I've put up with it long enough. Do you think I'm a dog in the house, an' not a man, do you –

MRS HOLROYD: A dog would be better.

HOLROYD: Oh! Oh! Then we'll see. We'll see who's the dog and who isna. We're goin' to see. [*He bangs the table.*]

MRS HOLROYD: Stop thumping that table! You've wakened those children once, you and your trollops.

HOLROYD: I shall do what the deuce I like!

MRS HOLROYD: No more, you won't, no more. I've stood this long enough. Now I'm going. As for you – you've got a red face where she slapped you. Now go to her.

HOLROYD: What? What?

MRS HOLROYD: For I'm sick of the sights and sounds of you.

HOLROYD [*bitterly*]: By God, an' I've known it a long time.

MRS HOLROYD: You have, and it's true.

HOLROYD: An' I know who it is th'rt hankerin' after.

MRS HOLROYD: I only want to be rid of you.

HOLROYD: I know it mighty well. But *I* know him!

[MRS HOLROYD, *sinking down on the sofa, suddenly begins to sob half-hysterically.* HOLROYD *watches her. As suddenly, she dries her eyes.*]

MRS HOLROYD: Do you think I care about what you say? [*Suddenly.*] Oh, I've had enough. I've tried, I've tried for years, for the children's sakes. Now I've had enough of your shame and disgrace.

HOLROYD: Oh, indeed!

MRS HOLROYD [*her voice is dull and inflexible*]: I've had enough. Go out again after those trollops – leave me alone. I've had enough.

[HOLROYD *stands looking at her.*]

Go, I mean it, go out again. And if you never come back again, I'm glad. I've had enough. [*She keeps her face averted, will not look at him, her attitude expressing thorough weariness.*]

HOLROYD: All right then! [*He hobbles, in unlaced boots, to the door. Then he turns to look at her. She turns herself still farther away, so that her back is towards him. He goes.*]

CURTAIN

ACT TWO

The scene is the same, two hours later. The cottage is in darkness, save for the firelight. On the table is spread a newspaper. A cup and saucer, a plate, a piece of bacon in the frying tin are on the newspaper ready for the miner's breakfast. MRS HOLROYD has gone to bed. There is a noise of heavy stumbling down the three steps outside.

BLACKMORE'S VOICE: Steady, now, steady. It's all in darkness. Missis! – Has she gone to bed? [*He tries the latch – shakes the door.*]

HOLROYD'S VOICE [*He is drunk*]: Her's locked me out. Let me smash that bloody door in. Come out – come out – ussza! [*He strikes a heavy blow on the door. There is a scuffle.*]

BLACKMORE'S VOICE: Hold on a bit – what're you doing?

HOLROYD'S VOICE: I'm smashing that blasted door in.

MRS HOLROYD [*appearing and suddenly drawing the bolts, flinging the door open*]: What do you think you're doing?

HOLROYD [*lurching into the room, snarling*]: What? What? Tha thought tha'd play thy monkey tricks on me, did ter? [*Shouting.*] But I'm going to show thee. [*He lurches at her threateningly; she recoils.*]

BLACKMORE [*seizing him by the arm*]: Here, here – ! Come and sit down and be quiet.

HOLROYD [*snarling at him*]: What? – What? An' what's thäigh got ter do wi' it. [*Shouting.*] What's thäigh got ter do wi' it?

BLACKMORE: Nothing – nothing; but it's getting late, and you want your supper.

HOLROYD [*shouting*]: I want nöwt. I'm allowed nöwt in this 'ouse. [*Shouting louder.*] 'Er begrudges me ivry morsel I ha'e.

MRS HOLROYD: Oh, what a story!

HOLROYD [*shouting*]: It's the truth, an' you know it.

BLACKMORE [*conciliatory*]: You'll rouse the children. You'll rouse the children, at this hour.

HOLROYD [*suddenly quiet*]: Not me – not if I know it. *I* shan't disturb 'em – bless 'em. [*He staggers to his arm-chair and sits heavily.*]

BLACKMORE: Shall I light the lamp?

MRS HOLROYD: No, don't trouble. Don't stay any longer, there's no need.

BLACKMORE [*quietly*]: I'll just see it's alright. [*He proceeds in silence to light the lamp.* HOLROYD *is seen dropping forward in his chair. He has a cut on his cheek.* MRS HOLROYD *is in an old-fashioned dressing-gown.* BLACKMORE *has an overcoat buttoned up to his chin. There is a very large lump of coal on the red fire.*]

MRS HOLROYD: Don't stay any longer.

BLACKMORE: I'll see it's alright.

MRS HOLROYD: I shall be all right. He'll go to sleep now.

BLACKMORE: But he can't go like that.

MRS HOLROYD: What has he done to his face?

BLACKMORE: He had a row with Jim Goodwin.

MRS HOLROYD: What about?

BLACKMORE: I don't know.

MRS HOLROYD: The beast!

BLACKMORE: By Jove, and isn't he a weight! He's getting fat, must be –

MRS HOLROYD: He's big made – he has a big frame.

BLACKMORE: Whatever he is, it took me all my time to get him home. I thought I'd better keep an eye on him. I knew you'd be worrying. So I sat in the smoke-room and waited for him. Though it's a dirty hole – and dull as hell.

MRS HOLROYD: Why did you bother?

BLACKMORE: Well, I thought you'd be upset about him. I had to drink three whiskies – had to, in all conscience – [*smiling*].

MRS HOLROYD: I don't want to be the ruin of you.

BLACKMORE [*smiling*]: Don't you? I thought he'd pitch forward on to the lines and crack his skull.

[HOLROYD *has been sinking farther and farther forward in drunken sleep. He suddenly jerks too far and is awakened. He sits upright, glaring fiercely and dazedly at the two, who instantly cease talking.*]

HOLROYD [*to* BLACKMORE]: What are thäigh doin' 'ere?

BLACKMORE: Why, I came along with you.

HOLROYD: Thou'rt a liar, I'm only just come in.

MRS HOLROYD [*coldly*]: He is no liar at all. He brought you home because you were too drunk to come yourself.

HOLROYD [*starting up*]: Thou'rt a liar! I niver set eyes on him this night, afore now.

MRS HOLROYD [*with a ' Pf' of contempt*]: You don't know what you *have* done to-night.

HOLROYD [*shouting*]: I s'll not ha'e it, I tell thee.

MRS HOLROYD: Psh!

HOLROYD: I s'll not ha'e it. I s'll ha'e no carryin's on i' my 'ouse –

MRS HOLROYD [*shrugging her shoulders*]: Talk when you've got some sense.

HOLROYD [*fiercely*]: I've as much sense as thäigh. Am I a fool? Canna I see? What's *he* doin' here then, answer me that. What – ?

MRS HOLROYD: Mr Blackmore came to bring *you* home because you were *too drunk* to find your own way. And this is the thanks he gets.

HOLROYD [*contemptuously*]: Blackymore, Blackymore. It's him tha cuts thy cloth by, is it?

MRS HOLROYD [*hotly*]: You don't know what you're talking about, so keep your tongue still.

HOLROYD [*bitingly*]: I don't know what I'm talking about – I don't know what I'm talking about – don't I? An' what about him standing there then, if I don't know what I'm talking about? – What?

BLACKMORE: You've been to sleep, Charlie, an' forgotten I came in with you, not long since.

HOLROYD: I'm not daft, I'm not a fool. I've got eyes in my head and sense. You needn't try to get over me. I know what you're up to.

BLACKMORE [*flushing*]: It's a bit off to talk to me like that, Charlie, I must say.

HOLROYD: I'm not good enough for 'er. She wants Mr Blackymore. He's a gentleman, he is. Now we have it all; now we understand.

MRS HOLROYD: I wish you understood enough to keep your tongue still.

HOLROYD: What? What? I'm to keep my tongue still, am I? An' what about *Mr Blackymore*?

MRS HOLROYD [*fiercely*]: Stop your mouth, you – you vulgar, low-minded brute.

HOLROYD: Am I? Am I? An' what are you? What tricks are you up to, an' all? But that's alright – that's alright. [*Shouting.*] That's alright, if it's *you*.

BLACKMORE: I think I'd better go. You seem to enjoy – er – er – calumniating your wife.

HOLROYD [*mockingly*]: Calamniating – calamniating – I'll give you calamniating, you mealy-mouthed jockey: I'll give you calamniating.

BLACKMORE: I think you've said about enough.

HOLROYD: 'Ave I, 'ave I? Yer flimsy jack – 'ave I? [*In a sudden burst.*] But I've not done wi' thee yet.

BLACKMORE [*ironically*]: No, and you haven't.

HOLROYD [*shouting – pulling himself up from the arm-chair*]: I'll show thee – I'll show thee.

[BLACKMORE *laughs.*]

HOLROYD: Yes! – yes, my young monkey. It's thäigh, is it?

BLACKMORE: Yes, it's *me*.

HOLROYD [*shouting*]: An' I'll ma'e thee wish it worn't, I will. What – ? What? Tha'd come slivin' round here, would ta? [*He lurches forward at* BLACKMORE *with clenched fist.*]

MRS HOLROYD: Drunken, drunken fool – oh, don't.

HOLROYD [*turning to her*]: What?

[*She puts up her hands before her face.* BLACKMORE *seizes the upraised arm and swings* HOLROYD *round.*]

BLACKMORE [*in a towering passion*]: Mind what tha'rt doing!

HOLROYD [*turning fiercely on him – incoherent*]: Wha' – wha' – !

[*He aims a heavy blow.* BLACKMORE *evades it, so that he is struck on the side of the chest. Suddenly he shows his teeth. He raises his fists ready to strike* HOLROYD *when the latter stands to advantage.*]

MRS HOLROYD [*rushing upon* BLACKMORE]: No, no! Oh, no! [*She flies and opens the door, and goes out.* BLACKMORE *glances after her, then at* HOLROYD, *who is preparing, like a bull, for another charge. The young man's face lights up.*]

HOLROYD: Wha' – wha' – ! [*As he advances,* BLACKMORE *quickly retreats out-of-doors.* HOLROYD *plunges upon him.* BLACKMORE *slips behind the door-jamb, puts out his foot, and trips* HOLROYD *with a crash upon the brick yard.*]

MRS HOLROYD: Oh, what has he done to himself?

BLACKMORE [*thickly*]: Tumbled over himself.

[HOLROYD *is seen struggling to rise, and is heard incoherently cursing.*]

MRS HOLROYD: Aren't you going to get him up?

BLACKMORE: What for?

MRS HOLROYD: But what shall we do?

BLACKMORE: Let him go to hell.

[HOLROYD, *who has subsided, begins to snarl and struggle again.*]

MRS HOLROYD [*in terror*]: He's getting up.

BLACKMORE: Alright, let him.

[MRS HOLROYD *looks at* BLACKMORE, *suddenly afraid of him also.*]

HOLROYD [*in a last frenzy*]: I'll show thee – I'll – [*He raises himself up, and is just picking his balance when* BLACKMORE, *with a sudden light kick, sends him sprawling again. He is seen on the edge of the light to collapse into stupor.*]

MRS HOLROYD: He'll kill you, he'll kill you!

[BLACKMORE *laughs short.*]

MRS HOLROYD: Would you believe it! Oh, isn't it awful! [*She begins to weep in a little hysteria;* BLACKMORE *stands with his back leaning on the doorway, grinning in a strained fashion.*] Is he hurt, do you think?

BLACKMORE: I don't know – I should think not.

MRS HOLROYD: I wish he was dead; I do, with all my heart.

BLACKMORE: Do you? [*He looks at her quickly; she wavers and shrinks; he begins to smile strainedly as before.*] You don't know *what* you wish, or what you want.

MRS HOLROYD [*troubled*]: Do you think I could get past him to come inside?

BLACKMORE: I should think so.

[MRS HOLROYD, *silent and troubled, manoeuvres in the door-way, stepping over her husband's feet, which lie on the threshold.*]

BLACKMORE: Why, you've got no shoes and stockings on!

MRS HOLROYD: No. [*She enters the house and stands trembling before the fire.*]

BLACKMORE [*following her*]: Are you cold?

MRS HOLROYD: A little – with standing on the yard.

BLACKMORE: What a shame!

[*She, uncertain of herself, sits down. He drops on one knee, awkwardly, and takes her feet in his hands.*]

MRS HOLROYD: Don't – no, don't!

BLACKMORE: They are frightfully cold. [*He remains, with head sunk, for some moments, then slowly rises.*] Damn him!

[*They look at each other; then, at the same time, turn away.*]

MRS HOLROYD: We can't leave him lying there.

BLACKMORE: No – no! I'll bring him in.

MRS HOLROYD: But – !

BLACKMORE: He won't wake again. The drink will have got hold of him by now. [*He hesitates.*] Could you take hold of his feet – he's so heavy.

MRS HOLROYD: Yes.

[*They go out and are seen stooping over* HOLROYD.]

BLACKMORE: Wait, wait, till I've got him – half a minute.

[MRS HOLROYD *backs in first. They carry* HOLROYD *in and lay him on the sofa.*]

MRS HOLROYD: Doesn't he look awful?

BLACKMORE: It's more mark than mar. It isn't much, really. [*He is busy taking off* HOLROYD'S *collar and tie, unfastening the waistcoat, the braces and the waist buttons of the trousers; he then proceeds to unlace the drunken man's boots.*]

MRS HOLROYD [*who has been watching closely*]: I shall never get him upstairs.

BLACKMORE: He can sleep here, with a rug or something to cover him. *You* don't want him – upstairs?

MRS HOLROYD: Never again.

BLACKMORE [*after a moment or two of silence*]: He'll be alright down here. Have you got a rug?

MRS HOLROYD: Yes. [*She goes upstairs.* BLACKMORE *goes into the scullery, returning with a ladling can and towel. He gets hot water from the boiler. Then, kneeling down, he begins to wipe the drunken man's face lightly with the flannel, to remove the blood and dirt.*]

MRS HOLROYD [*returning*]: What are you doing?

BLACKMORE: Only wiping his face to get the dirt out.

MRS HOLROYD: I wonder if he'd do as much for you.

BLACKMORE: I hope not.

MRS HOLROYD: Isn't he horrible, horrible –

BLACKMORE [*looks up at her*]: Don't look at him then.

MRS HOLROYD: I can't take it in, it's too much.

BLACKMORE: He won't wake. I will stay with you.

MRS HOLROYD [*earnestly*]: No – oh, no.

BLACKMORE: There will be the drawn sword between us. [*He indicates the figure of* HOLROYD, *which lies, in effect, as a barrier between them.*]

MRS HOLROYD [*blushing*]: Don't!

BLACKMORE: I'm sorry.

MRS HOLROYD [*after watching him for a few moments lightly wiping the sleeping man's face with a towel*]: I wonder you can be so careful over him.

BLACKMORE [*quietly*]: It's only because he's helpless.

MRS HOLROYD: But why should you love him ever so little?

BLACKMORE: I don't – only he's helpless. Five minutes since I could have killed him.

MRS HOLROYD: Well, I don't understand you men.

BLACKMORE: Why?

MRS HOLROYD: I don't know.

BLACKMORE: I thought as I stood in that doorway, and he was trying to get up – I wished as hard as I've ever wished anything in my life –

MRS HOLROYD: What?

BLACKMORE: That I'd killed him. I've never wished anything so much in my life – if wishes were anything.

MRS HOLROYD: Don't, it *does* sound awful.

BLACKMORE: I *could* have done it, too. He ought to be dead.

MRS HOLROYD [*pleading*]: No, don't! You know you don't mean it, and you make me feel so awful.

BLACKMORE: I do mean it. It is simply true, what I say.

MRS HOLROYD: But don't say it.

BLACKMORE: No?

MRS HOLROYD: No, we've had enough.

BLACKMORE: Give me the rug.

[*She hands it him, and he tucks* HOLROYD *up.*]

MRS HOLROYD: You only do it to play on my feelings.

BLACKMORE [*laughing shortly*]: And now give me a pillow – thanks.

[*There is a pause – both look at the sleeping man.*]

BLACKMORE: I suppose you're fond of him, really.

MRS HOLROYD: No more.

BLACKMORE: You *were* fond of him?

MRS HOLROYD: I was – yes.

BLACKMORE: What did you like in him?

MRS HOLROYD [*uneasily*]: I don't know.

BLACKMORE: I suppose you really care about him, even now?

MRS HOLROYD: Why are you so sure of it?

BLACKMORE: Because I think it is so.

MRS HOLROYD: I did care for him – now he has destroyed it –

BLACKMORE: I don't believe he can destroy it.

MRS HOLROYD [*with a short laugh*]: Don't you? When you are married you try. You'll find it isn't so hard.

BLACKMORE: But what did you like in him – because he was good-looking, and strong, and that?

MRS HOLROYD: I liked that as well. But if a man makes a nuisance of himself, his good looks are ugly to you, and his strength loathsome. Do you think I *care* about a man because he's got big fists, when he is a coward in his real self?

BLACKMORE: Is he a coward?

MRS HOLROYD: He *is* – a pettifogging, paltry one.

BLACKMORE: And so you've really done with him?

MRS HOLROYD: I have.

BLACKMORE: And what are you going to do?

MRS HOLROYD: I don't know.

BLACKMORE: I suppose nothing. You'll just go on – even if you've done with him – you'll go on with him.

[*There is a long pause.*]

BLACKMORE: But was there nothing else in him but his muscles and his good looks to attract you to him?

MRS HOLROYD: Why? What does it matter?

BLACKMORE: What did you *think* he was?

MRS HOLROYD: Why must we talk about him?

BLACKMORE: Because I can never quite believe you.

MRS HOLROYD: I can't help whether you believe it or not.

BLACKMORE: Are you just in a rage with him, because of to-night?

MRS HOLROYD: I know, to-night finished it. But it was never right between us.

BLACKMORE: Never?

MRS HOLROYD: Not once. And then to-night – no, it's too much; I can't stand any more of it.

BLACKMORE: I suppose he got tipsy. Then he said he wasn't a married man – vowed he wasn't, to those paper bonnets. They found out he was, and said he was frightened of his wife getting to know. Then he said they should all go to supper at his house – I suppose they came out of mischief.

MRS HOLROYD: He did it to insult me.

BLACKMORE: Oh, he was a bit tight – you can't say it was deliberate.

MRS HOLROYD: No, but it shows how he feels toward me. The feeling comes out in drink.

BLACKMORE: How does he feel toward you?

MRS HOLROYD: He wants to insult me, and humiliate me, in every moment of his life. Now I simply despise him.

BLACKMORE: You really don't care any more about him?

MRS HOLROYD: No.

BLACKMORE [*hesitates*]: And you would leave him?

MRS HOLROYD: I would leave him, and not care *that* about him any more. [*She snaps her fingers.*]

BLACKMORE: Will you come with me?

MRS HOLROYD [*after a reluctant pause*]: Where?

BLACKMORE: To Spain: I can any time have a job there, in a decent part. You could take the children.

[*The figure of the sleeper stirs uneasily – they watch him.*]

BLACKMORE: Will you?

MRS HOLROYD: When would you go?

BLACKMORE: To-morrow, if you like.

MRS HOLROYD: But why do you want to saddle yourself with me and the children?

BLACKMORE: Because I want to.

MRS HOLROYD: But you don't love me?

BLACKMORE: Why don't I?

MRS HOLROYD: You don't.

BLACKMORE: I don't know about that. I don't know anything about love. Only I've gone on for a year, now, and it's got stronger and stronger –

MRS HOLROYD: What has?

BLACKMORE: This – this wanting you, to live with me. I took no notice of it for a long time. Now I can't get away from it, at no hour and nohow. [*He still avoids direct contact with her.*]

MRS HOLROYD: But you'd *like* to get away from it.

BLACKMORE: I hate a mess of any sort. But if you'll come away with me – you and the children –

MRS HOLROYD: But I couldn't – you don't love me –

BLACKMORE: I don't know what you mean by I don't love you.

MRS HOLROYD: I can feel it.

BLACKMORE: And do you love *me*? [*A pause.*]

MRS HOLROYD: I don't know. Everything is so – so –
   [*There is a long pause.*]

BLACKMORE: How old are you?

MRS HOLROYD: Thirty-two.

BLACKMORE: I'm twenty-seven.

MRS HOLROYD: And have you never been in love?

BLACKMORE: I don't think so. I don't know.

MRS HOLROYD: But you must know. I must go and shut that door that keeps clicking. [*She rises to go upstairs, making a clatter at the stairfoot door. The noise rouses her husband. As she goes upstairs, he moves, makes coughing sounds, turns over, and then suddenly sits upright, gazing at* BLACKMORE. *The latter sits perfectly still on the sofa, his head dropped, hiding his face. His hands are clasped. They remain thus for a minute.*]

HOLROYD: Hello! [*He stares fixedly.*] Hello! [*His tone is un-decided, as if he mistrusts himself.*] What are — who are ter? [BLACKMORE *does not move;* HOLROYD *stares blankly; he then turns and looks at the room.*] Well, I dunna know. [*He staggers to his feet, clinging to the table, and goes groping to the stairs. They creak loudly under his weight. A door-latch is heard to click. In a moment* MRS HOLROYD *comes quickly downstairs.*]

BLACKMORE: Has he gone to bed?

MRS HOLROYD [*nodding*]: Lying on the bed.

BLACKMORE: Will he settle now?

MRS HOLROYD: I don't know. He is like that sometimes. He will have delirium tremens if he goes on.

BLACKMORE [*softly*]: You can't stay with him, you know.

MRS HOLROYD: And the children?

BLACKMORE: We'll take them.

MRS HOLROYD: Oh! [*Her face puckers to cry. Suddenly he starts up and puts his arms round her, holding her protectively and gently, very caressingly. She clings to him. They are silent for some moments.*]

BLACKMORE [*struggling, in an altered voice*]: Look at me and kiss me.

[*Her sobs are heard distinctly.* BLACKMORE *lays his hand on her cheek, caressing her always with his hand.*]

BLACKMORE: My God, but I hate him! I wish either he was dead or me.

[MRS HOLROYD *hides against him; her sobs cease; after a while he continues in the same murmuring fashion.*]

It can't go on like it any more. I feel as if I should come in two. I can't keep away from you. I simply can't. Come with me. Come with me and leave him. If you knew what a hell it is for me to have you here — and to see him. I can't go without you, I can't. It's been hell every moment for six months now. You say I don't love you. Perhaps I don't, for all I know about it. But oh, my God, don't keep me like it any longer. Why should *he* have you – and I've never had anything.

MRS HOLROYD: Have you never loved anybody?

BLACKMORE: No – I've tried. Kiss me of your own wish – will you?

MRS HOLROYD: I don't know.

BLACKMORE [*after a pause*]: Let's break clear. Let's go right away. Do you care for me?

MRS HOLROYD: I don't know. [*She loosens herself, rises dumbly.*]

BLACKMORE: When do you think you *will* know?
[*She sits down helplessly.*]

MRS HOLROYD: I don't know.

BLACKMORE: Yes, you do know, really. If he was dead, should you marry me?

MRS HOLROYD: Don't say it –

BLACKMORE: Why not? If wishing of mine would kill him, he'd soon be out of the way.

MRS HOLROYD: But the children!

BLACKMORE: I'm fond of them. I shall have good money.

MRS HOLROYD: But he's their father.

BLACKMORE: What does that mean – ?

MRS HOLROYD: Yes, I know – [*a pause*] but –

BLACKMORE: Is it *him* that keeps you?

MRS HOLROYD: No.

BLACKMORE: Then come with me. Will you? [*He stands waiting for her; then he turns and takes his overcoat; pulls it on, leaving the collar turned up, ceasing to twist his cap.*] Well – will you tell me to-morrow?
[*She goes forward and flings her arms round his neck. He suddenly kisses her passionately.*]

MRS HOLROYD: But I ought not. [*She draws away a little; he will not let her go.*]

BLACKMORE: Yes, it's alright. [*He holds her close.*]

MRS HOLROYD: Is it?

BLACKMORE: Yes, it is. It's alright. [*He kisses her again. She releases herself but holds his hand. They keep listening.*]

MRS HOLROYD: Do you love me?

BLACKMORE: What do you ask for?

MRS HOLROYD: Have I hurt you these months?

BLACKMORE: *You* haven't. And I don't care what it's been if you'll come with me. [*There is a noise upstairs and they wait.*] You *will* soon, won't you?

    [*She kisses him.*]

MRS HOLROYD: He's not safe. [*She disengages herself and sits on the sofa.*]

BLACKMORE [*takes a place beside her, holding her hand in both his*]: You should have waited for me.

MRS HOLROYD: How wait?

BLACKMORE: And not have married him.

MRS HOLROYD: I might never have known you – I married him to get out of my place.

BLACKMORE: Why?

MRS HOLROYD: I was left an orphan when I was six. My Uncle John brought me up, in the Coach and Horses at Rainsworth. He'd got no children. He was good to me, but he drank. I went to Mansfield Grammar School. Then he fell out with me because I wouldn't wait in the bar, and I went as nursery governess to Berryman's. And I felt I'd nowhere to go, I belonged to nowhere, and nobody cared about me, and men came after me, and I hated it. So to get out of it, I married the first man that turned up.

BLACKMORE: And you never cared about him?

MRS HOLROYD: Yes, I did. I did care about him. I wanted to be a wife to him. But there's nothing at the bottom of him, if you know what I mean. You can't *get* anywhere with him. There's just his body and nothing else. Nothing that keeps him, no anchor, no roots, nothing satisfying. It's a horrible feeling there is about him, that nothing is safe or permanent – nothing is anything –

BLACKMORE: And do you think you can trust *me*?

MRS HOLROYD: I think you're different from him.

BLACKMORE: Perhaps I'm not.

MRS HOLROYD [*warmly*]: You are.

BLACKMORE: At any rate, we'll see. You'll come on Saturday to London?

MRS HOLROYD: Well, you see, there's my money. I haven't

got it yet. My uncle has left me about a hundred and twenty pounds.

BLACKMORE: Well, see the lawyer about it as soon as you can. I can let you have some money if you want any. But don't let us wait after Saturday.

MRS HOLROYD: But isn't it wrong?

BLACKMORE: Why, if you don't care for him, and the children are miserable between the two of you – which they are –

MRS HOLROYD: Yes.

BLACKMORE: Well, then I see no wrong. As for him – he would go one way, and only one way, whatever you do. Damn him, he doesn't matter.

MRS HOLROYD: No.

BLACKMORE: Well, then – have done with it. Can't you cut clean of him? Can't you now?

MRS HOLROYD: And then – the children –

BLACKMORE: They'll be alright with me and you – won't they?

MRS HOLROYD: Yes –

BLACKMORE: Well, then. Now, come and have done with it. We can't keep on being ripped in two like this. We need never hear of him any more.

MRS HOLROYD: Yes – I love you. I do love you –

BLACKMORE: Oh, my God! [*He speaks with difficulty – embracing her.*]

MRS HOLROYD: When I look at him, and then at you – ha – [*She gives a short laugh.*]

BLACKMORE: He's had all the chance – it's only fair – Lizzie –

MRS HOLROYD: My love.

[*There is silence. He keeps his arm round her. After hesitating, he picks up his cap.*]

BLACKMORE: I'll go then – at any rate. Shall you come with me?

[*She follows him to the door.*]

MRS HOLROYD: I'll come on Saturday.

BLACKMORE: Not now?

CURTAIN

ACT THREE

Scene, the same. Time, the following evening, about seven o'clock. The table is half-laid, with a large cup and saucer, plate, etc., ready for HOLROYD'S *dinner, which, like all miners, he has when he comes home between four and five o'clock. On the other half of the table* MRS HOLROYD *is ironing. On the hearth stand newly baked loaves of bread. The irons hang at the fire.* JACK, *with a bowler hat hanging at the back of his head, parades up to the sofa, on which stands* MINNIE *engaged in dusting a picture. She has a soiled white apron tied behind her, to make a long skirt.*

JACK: Good mornin', missis. Any scissors or knives to grind?

MINNIE [*peering down from the sofa*]: Oh, I can't be bothered to come downstairs. Call another day.

JACK: I shan't.

MINNIE [*keeping up her part*]: Well, I can't come down now. [JACK *stands irresolute.*] Go on, you have to go and steal the baby.

JACK: I'm not.

MINNIE: Well, you can steal the eggs out of the fowl-house.

JACK: I'm not.

MINNIE: Then I shan't play with you.

[JACK *takes off his bowler hat and flings it on the sofa; tears come in* MINNIE'S *eyes.*]

Now I'm *not* friends. [*She surveys him ruefully; after a few moments of silence she clambers down and goes to her mother.*] Mam, he won't play with me.

MRS HOLROYD [*crossly*]: Why don't you play with her? If you begin bothering, you must go to bed.

JACK: Well, I don't want to play.

MRS HOLROYD: Then you must go to bed.

JACK: I don't want to.

MRS HOLROYD: Then what do you want, I should like to know?

MINNIE: I wish my father'd come.

JACK: I do.

MRS HOLROYD: I suppose he thinks he's paying me out. This is the third time this week he's slunk past the door and gone down to Old Brinsley instead of coming in to his dinner. He'll be as drunk as a lord when he does come.

[*The children look at her plaintively.*]

MINNIE: Isn't he a nuisance?

JACK: I hate him. I wish he'd drop down th' pit-shaft.

MRS HOLROYD: Jack! – I never heard such a thing in my life! You mustn't say such things – it's wicked.

JACK: Well, I do.

MRS HOLROYD [*loudly*]: I won't have it. He's your father, remember.

JACK [*in a high voice*]: Well, he's always comin' home an' shoutin' an' bangin' on the table. [*He is getting tearful and defiant.*]

MRS HOLROYD: Well, you mustn't take any notice of him.

MINNIE [*wistfully*]: 'Appen if you said something nice to him, mother, he'd happen go to bed, and not shout.

JACK: I'd hit him in the mouth.

MRS HOLROYD: Perhaps we'll go to another country, away from him – should we?

JACK: In a ship, mother?

MINNIE: In a ship, mam?

MRS HOLROYD: Yes, in a big ship, where it's blue sky, and water and palm-trees, and –

MINNIE: An' dates – ?

JACK: When should we go?

MRS HOLROYD: Some day.

MINNIE: But who'd work for us? Who should we have for father?

JACK: You don't want a father. I can go to work for us.

MRS HOLROYD: I've got a lot of money now, that your uncle left me.

MINNIE [*after a general thoughtful silence*]: An' would my father stop here?

MRS HOLROYD: Oh, he'd be alright.

MINNIE: But who would he live with?

183

MRS HOLROYD: I don't know – one of his paper bonnets, if he likes.

MINNIE: Then she could have her old bracelet back, couldn't she?

MRS HOLROYD: Yes – there it is on the candlestick, waiting for her.

[*There is a sound of footsteps – then a knock at the door. The children start.*]

MINNIE [*in relief*]: Here he is.

[MRS HOLROYD *goes to the door.* BLACKMORE *enters.*]

BLACKMORE: It is foggy to-night – Hello, aren't you youngsters gone to bed?

MINNIE: No, my father's not come home yet.

BLACKMORE [*turning to* MRS HOLROYD]: Did he go to work then, after last night?

MRS HOLROYD: I suppose so. His pit things were gone when I got up. I never thought he'd go.

BLACKMORE: And he took his snap as usual?

MRS HOLROYD: Yes, just as usual. I suppose he's gone to the New Inn. He'd say to himself he'd pay me out. That's what he always does say, 'I'll pay thee out for that bit – I'll ma'e thee regret it.'

JACK: We're going to leave him.

BLACKMORE: So you think he's at the New Inn?

MRS HOLROYD: I'm sure he is – and he'll come when he's full. He'll have a bout now, you'll see.

MINNIE: Go and fetch him, Mr Blackmore.

JACK: My mother says we shall go in a ship and leave him.

BLACKMORE [*after looking keenly at* JACK: *to* MRS HOLROYD]: Shall I go and see if he's at the New Inn?

MRS HOLROYD: No – perhaps you'd better not –

BLACKMORE: Oh, he shan't see me. I can easily manage that.

JACK: Fetch him, Mr Blackmore.

BLACKMORE: Alright, Jack. [*To* MRS HOLROYD.] Shall I?

MRS HOLROYD: We're always pulling on you – But yes, do!

[BLACKMORE *goes out.*]

JACK: I wonder how long he'll be.

MRS HOLROYD: You come and go to bed now: you'd better be out of the way when he comes in.

MINNIE: And you won't say anything to him, mother, will you?

MRS HOLROYD: What do you mean?

MINNIE: You won't begin of him – row him.

MRS HOLROYD: Is he to have all his own way? What *would* he be like, if I didn't row him?

JACK: But it doesn't matter, mother, if we're going to leave him –

MINNIE: But Mr Blackmore'll come back, won't he, mam, and dad won't shout before him?

MRS HOLROYD [*beginning to undress the children*]: Yes, he'll come back.

MINNIE: Mam – could I have that bracelet to go to bed with?

MRS HOLROYD: Come and say your prayers.

[*They kneel, muttering in their mother's apron.*]

MINNIE [*suddenly lifting her head*]: Can I, mam?

MRS HOLROYD [*trying to be stern*]: Have you finished your prayers?

MINNIE: Yes.

MRS HOLROYD: If you want it – beastly thing! [*She reaches the bracelet down from the mantelpiece.*] Your father must have put it up there – I don't know where I left it. I suppose he'd think I was proud of it and wanted it for an ornament.

[MINNIE *gloats over it.* MRS HOLROYD *lights a candle and they go upstairs. After a few moments the outer door opens, and there enters an old woman. She is of middling stature and wears a large grey shawl over her head. After glancing sharply round the room, she advances to the fire, warms herself, then, taking off her shawl, sits in the rocking-chair. As she hears* MRS HOLROYD'S *footsteps, she folds her hands and puts on a lachrymose expression, turning down the corners of her mouth and arching her eyebrows.*]

MRS HOLROYD: Hello, mother, is it you?

GRANDMOTHER: Yes, it's me. Haven't you finished ironing?

MRS HOLROYD: Not yet.

GRANDMOTHER: You'll have your irons red-hot.

MRS HOLROYD: Yes, I s'll have to stand them to cool. [*She does so, and moves about at her ironing.*]

GRANDMOTHER: And you don't know what's become of Charles?

MRS HOLROYD: Well, he's not come home from work yet. I supposed he was at the New Inn – Why?

GRANDMOTHER: That young electrician come knocking asking if I knew where he was. 'Eh,' I said, 'I've not set eyes on him for over a week – nor his wife neither, though they pass th' garden gate every time they go out. I know nowt on 'im.' I axed him what was the matter, so he said Mrs Holroyd was anxious because he'd not come home, so I thought I'd better come and see. Is there anything up?

MRS HOLROYD: No more than I've told you.

GRANDMOTHER: It's a rum 'un, if he's neither in the New Inn nor the Prince o' Wales. I suppose something you've done's set him off.

MRS HOLROYD: It's nothing I've done.

GRANDMOTHER: Eh, if he's gone off and left you, whativer shall we do! Whativer 'ave you been doing?

MRS HOLROYD: He brought a couple of bright daisies here last night – two of those trollops from Nottingham – and I said I'd not have it.

GRANDMOTHER [*sighing deeply*]: Ay, you've never been able to agree.

MRS HOLROYD: We agreed well enough except when he drank like a fish and came home rolling.

GRANDMOTHER [*whining*]: Well, what can you expect of a man as 'as been shut up i' th' pit all day? He must have a bit of relaxation.

MRS HOLROYD: He can have it different from that, then. At any rate, I'm sick of it.

GRANDMOTHER: Ay, you've a stiff neck, but it'll be bowed by you're my age.

MRS HOLROYD: Will it? I'd rather it were broke.

GRANDMOTHER: Well – there's no telling what a jealous man will do. [*She shakes her head.*]

MRS HOLROYD: Nay, I think it's my place to be jealous, when

he brings a brazen hussy here and sits carryin' on with her.

GRANDMOTHER: He'd no business to do that. But you know, Lizzie, he's got something on *his* side.

MRS HOLROYD: What, pray?

GRANDMOTHER: Well, I don't want to make any mischief, but you're my son's wife, an' it's nothing but my duty to tell you. They've been saying a long time now as that young electrician is here a bit too often.

MRS HOLROYD: He doesn't come for my asking.

GRANDMOTHER: No, I don't suppose he wants for asking. But Charlie's not the man to put up with that sort o' work.

MRS HOLROYD: Charlie put up with it! If he's anything to say, why doesn't he say it, without going to other folks . . . ?

GRANDMOTHER: Charlie's never been near me with a word – nor 'as he said a word elsewhere to my knowledge. For all that, this is going to end with trouble.

MRS HOLROYD: In this hole, every gossiping creature thinks she's got the right to cackle about you – sickening! And a parcel of lies.

GRANDMOTHER: Well, Lizzie, I've never said anything against you. Charlie's been a handful of trouble. He made my heart ache once or twice afore you had him, and he's made it ache many, many's the time since. But it's not all on his side, you know.

MRS HOLROYD [*hotly*]: No, I don't know.

GRANDMOTHER: You thought yourself above him, Lizzie, an' you know he's not the man to stand it.

MRS HOLROYD: No, he's run away from it.

GRANDMOTHER [*venomously*]: And what man wouldn't leave a woman that allowed him to live on sufferance in the house with her, when he was bringing the money home?

MRS HOLROYD: 'Sufferance!' – Yes, there's been a lot of letting him live on 'sufferance' in the house with me. It is *I* who have lived on sufferance, for his service and pleasure. No, what he wanted was the drink and the public house company, and because he couldn't get them here, he went out for them. That's all.

GRANDMOTHER: You have always been very clever at hitting things off, Lizzie. I was always sorry my youngest son married a clever woman. He only wanted a bit of coaxing and managing, and you clever women won't do it.

MRS HOLROYD: He wanted a slave, not a wife.

GRANDMOTHER: It's a pity your stomach wasn't too high for him, before you had him. But no, you could have eaten him ravishing at one time.

MRS HOLROYD: It's a pity you didn't tell me what he was before I had him. But no, he was all angel. You left me to find out what he really was.

GRANDMOTHER: Some women could have lived with him happy enough. An' a fat lot you'd have thanked me for my telling.

[*There is a knock at the door.* MRS HOLROYD *opens.*]

RIGLEY: They tell me, missus, as your mester's not hoom yet.

MRS HOLROYD: No – who is it?

GRANDMOTHER: Ask him to step inside. Don't stan' there lettin' the fog in.

[RIGLEY *steps in. He is a tall, bony, very roughly hewn collier.*]

RIGLEY: Good evenin'.

GRANDMOTHER: Oh, is it you, Mr Rigley? [*In a querulous, spiteful tone to* MRS HOLROYD.] He butties along with Charlie.

MRS HOLROYD: Oh!

RIGLEY: An' han yer seen nowt on 'im?

MRS HOLROYD: No – was he all right at work?

RIGLEY: Well, 'e wor nowt to mention. A bit short, like: 'adna much to say. I canna ma'e out what 'e's done wi' 'issen. [*He is manifestly uneasy, does not look at the two women.*]

GRANDMOTHER: An' did 'e come up i' th' same bantle wi' you?

RIGLEY: No – 'e didna. As Ah was comin' out o' th' stall, Ah shouted, 'Art comin', Charlie? We're a' off.' An' 'e said, 'Ah'm comin' in a minute.' 'E wor just finishin' a stint, like, an' 'e wanted ter get it set. An' 'e 'd been a bit roughish in' is temper, like, so I thöwt 'e didna want ter walk to th' bottom wi' us. . . .

GRANDMOTHER [*wailing*]: An' what's 'e gone an' done to himself?

RIGLEY: Nay, missis, yo munna ax me that. 'E's non done owt as Ah know on. On'y I wor thinkin', 'appen summat 'ad 'appened to 'im, like, seein' as nob'dy had any knowings of 'im comin' up.

MRS HOLROYD: What is the matter, Mr Rigley? Tell us it out.

RIGLEY: I canna do that, missis. It seems as if 'e niver come up th' pit – as far as we can make out. 'Appen a bit o' stuff's fell an' pinned 'im.

GRANDMOTHER [*wailing*]: An' 'ave you left 'im lying down there in the pit, poor thing?

RIGLEY [*uneasily*]: I couldna say for certain where 'e is.

MRS HOLROYD [*agitated*]: Oh, it's very likely not very bad, mother! Don't let us run to meet trouble.

RIGLEY: We 'ave to 'ope for th' best, missis, all on us.

GRANDMOTHER [*wailing*]: Eh, they'll bring 'im 'ome, I know they will, smashed up an' broke! An' one of my sons they've burned down pit till the flesh dropped off 'im, an' one was shot till 'is shoulder was all of a mosh, an' they brought 'em 'ome to me. An' now there's this. . . .

MRS HOLROYD [*shuddering*]: Oh, don't mother. [*Appealing to* RIGLEY.] You don't know that he's hurt?

RIGLEY [*shaking his head*]: I canna tell you.

MRS HOLROYD [*in a high hysterical voice*]: Then what is it?

RIGLEY [*very uneasy*]: I canna tell you. But yon young electrician – Mr Blackmore – 'e rung down to the night deputy, an' it seems as though there's been a fall or summat. . . .

GRANDMOTHER: Eh, Lizzie, you parted from him in anger. You little knowed how you'd meet him again.

RIGLEY [*making an effort*]: Well, I'd 'appen best be goin' to see what's betide. [*He goes out.*]

GRANDMOTHER: I'm sure I've had my share of bad luck, I have. I'm sure I've brought up five lads in the pit, through accidents and troubles, and now there's this. The Lord has treated me very hard, very hard. It's a blessing, Lizzie, as you've got a bit of money, else what would 'ave become of the children?

MRS HOLROYD: Well, if he's badly hurt, there'll be the Union-pay, and sick-pay – we shall manage. And perhaps it's *not* very much.

GRANDMOTHER: There's no knowin' but what they'll be carryin' him to die i' th' hospital.

MRS HOLROYD: Oh, don't say so, mother – it won't be so bad, you'll see.

GRANDMOTHER: How much money have you, Lizzie, comin'?

MRS HOLROYD: I don't know – not much over a hundred pounds.

GRANDMOTHER [*shaking her head*]: An' what's that, what's that?

MRS HOLROYD [*sharply*]: Hush!

GRANDMOTHER [*crying*]: Why, what?

[MRS HOLROYD *opens the door. In the silence can be heard the pulsing of the fan engine, then the driving engine chuffs rapidly: there is a skirr of brakes on the rope as it descends.*]

MRS HOLROYD: That's twice they've sent the chair down – I wish we could see. . . . Hark!

GRANDMOTHER: What is it?

MRS HOLROYD: Yes – it's stopped at the gate. It's the doctor's.

GRANDMOTHER [*coming to the door*]: What, Lizzie?

MRS HOLROYD: The doctor's motor. [*She listens acutely.*] Dare you stop here, mother, while I run up to the top an' see?

GRANDMOTHER: You'd better not go, Lizzie, you'd better not. A woman's best away.

MRS HOLROYD: It is unbearable to wait.

GRANDMOTHER: Come in an' shut the door – it's a cold that gets in your bones.

[MRS HOLROYD *goes in.*]

MRS HOLROYD: Perhaps while he's in bed we shall have time to change him. It's an ill wind brings no good. He'll happen be a better man.

GRANDMOTHER: Well, you can but try. Many a woman's thought the same.

MRS HOLROYD: Oh, dear, I wish somebody would come. He's never been hurt since we were married.

GRANDMOTHER: No, he's never had a bad accident, all the years he's been in the pit. He's been luckier than most. But everybody has it, sooner or later.

MRS HOLROYD [*shivering*]: It *is* a horrid night.

GRANDMOTHER [*querulous*]: Yes, come your ways in.

MRS HOLROYD: Hark!

[*There is a quick sound of footsteps.* BLACKMORE *comes into the light of the doorway.*]

BLACKMORE: They're bringing him.

MRS HOLROYD [*quickly putting her hand over her breast*]: What is it?

BLACKMORE: You can't tell anything's the matter with him – it's not marked him at all.

MRS HOLROYD: Oh, what a blessing! And is it much?

BLACKMORE: Well –

MRS HOLROYD: What is it?

BLACKMORE: It's the worst.

GRANDMOTHER: Who is it? – What does he say?

[MRS HOLROYD *sinks on the nearest chair with a horrified expression.* BLACKMORE *pulls himself together and enters the room. He is very pale.*]

BLACKMORE: I came to tell you they're bringing him home.

GRANDMOTHER: And you said it wasn't very bad, did you?

BLACKMORE: No – I said it was – as bad as it could be.

MRS HOLROYD [*rising and crossing to her* MOTHER-IN-LAW, *flings her arms round her; in a high voice*]: Oh, mother, what shall we do? What shall we do?

GRANDMOTHER: You don't mean to say he's dead?

BLACKMORE: Yes.

GRANDMOTHER [*staring*]: God help us, and how was it?

BLACKMORE: Some stuff fell.

GRANDMOTHER [*rocking herself and her daughter-in-law – both weeping*]: Oh, God have mercy on us! Oh, God have mercy on us! Some stuff fell on him. An' he'd not even time to cry for mercy; oh, God spare him! Oh, what shall we do for comfort? To be taken straight out of his sins. Oh, Lizzie, to think he should be cut off in his wickedness! He's been a bad lad of late, he has, poor lamb. He's gone

very wrong of late years, poor dear lamb, very wrong. Oh,
Lizzie, think what's to become of him now! If only you'd
have tried to be different with him.

MRS HOLROYD [*moaning*]: Don't, mother, don't. I can't bear
it.

BLACKMORE [*cold and clear*]: Where will you have him laid?
The men will be here in a moment.

MRS HOLROYD [*starting up*]: They can carry him up to bed –

BLACKMORE: It's no good taking him upstairs. You'll have
to wash him and lay him out.

MRS HOLROYD [*startled*]: Well –

BLACKMORE: He's in his pit-dirt.

GRANDMOTHER: He is, bless him. We'd better have him
down here, Lizzie, where we can handle him.

MRS HOLROYD: Yes. [*She begins to put the tea things away, but
drops the sugar out of the basin and the lumps fly broadcast.*]

BLACKMORE: Never mind, I'll pick those up. You put the
children's clothes away.

[MRS HOLROYD *stares witless around. The* GRANDMOTHER
sits rocking herself and weeping. BLACKMORE *clears the table,
putting the pots in the scullery. He folds the white tablecloth and
pulls back the table. The door opens.* MRS HOLROYD *utters a
cry.* RIGLEY *enters.*]

RIGLEY: They're bringing him now, missis.

MRS HOLROYD: Oh!

RIGLEY [*simply*]: There must ha' been a fall directly after we
left him.

MRS HOLROYD [*frowning, horrified*]: No – no!

RIGLEY [*to* BLACKMORE]: It fell a' back of him, an' shut 'im
in as you might shut a loaf i' th' oven. It never touched him.

MRS HOLROYD [*staring distractedly*]: Well, then –

RIGLEY: You see, it come on 'im as close as a trap on a
mouse, an' gen him no air, an' what wi' th' gas, it smothered
him. An' it wouldna be so very long about it neither.

MRS HOLROYD [*quiet with horror*]: Oh!

GRANDMOTHER: Eh, dear – dear. Eh, dear – dear.

RIGLEY [*looking hard at her*]: I wasna to know what 'ud
happen.

GRANDMOTHER [*not heeding him, but weeping all the time*]: But the Lord gave him time to repent. He'd have a few minutes to repent. Ay, I hope he did, I hope he did, else what was to become of him. The Lord cut him off in his sins, but He gave him time to repent.

[RIGLEY *looks away at the wall.* BLACKMORE *has made a space in the middle of the floor.*]

BLACKMORE: If you'll take the rocking-chair off the end of the rug, Mrs Holroyd, I can pull it back a bit from the fire, and we can lay him on that.

GRANDMOTHER [*petulantly*]: What's the good of messing about – [*She moves.*]

MRS HOLROYD: It suffocated him?

RIGLEY [*shaking his head, briefly*]: Yes. 'Appened th' after-damp –

BLACKMORE: He'd be dead in a few minutes.

MRS HOLROYD: No – oh, think!

BLACKMORE: You mustn't think.

RIGLEY [*suddenly*]: They commin'!

[MRS HOLROYD *stands at bay. The* GRANDMOTHER *half rises.* RIGLEY *and* BLACKMORE *efface themselves as much as possible. A man backs into the room, bearing the feet of the dead man, which are shod in great pit boots. As the head bearer comes awkwardly past the table, the coat with which the body is covered slips off, revealing* HOLROYD *in his pit-dirt, naked to the waist.*]

MANAGER [*a little stout, white-bearded man*]: Mind now, mind. Ay, missis, what a job, indeed, it is! [*Sharply*] Where mun they put him?

MRS HOLROYD [*turning her face aside from the corpse*]: Lay him on the rug.

MANAGER: Steady now, do it steady.

SECOND BEARER [*rising and pressing back his shoulders*]: By Guy, but 'e 'ings heavy.

MANAGER: Yi, Joe, I'll back my life o' that.

GRANDMOTHER: Eh, Mr Chambers, what's this affliction on my old age. You kept your sons out o' the pit, but all mine's in. And to think of the trouble I've had – to think o' the trouble that's come out of Brinsley pit to me.

MANAGER: It has that, it 'as that, missis. You seem to have had more'n your share; I'll admit it, you have.

MRS HOLROYD [*who has been staring at the men*]: It is too much!
 [BLACKMORE *frowns;* RIGLEY *glowers at her.*]

MANAGER: You never knowed such a thing in your life. Here's a man, holin' a stint, just finishin', [*He puts himself as if in the holer's position, gesticulating freely.*] an' a lot o' stuff falls behind him, clean as a whistle, shuts him up safe as a worm in a nut and niver touches him – niver knowed such a thing in your life.

MRS HOLROYD: Ugh!

MANAGER: It niver hurt him – niver touched him.

MRS HOLROYD: Yes, but – but how long would he be [*She makes a sweeping gesture; the* MANAGER *looks at her and will not help her out.*] – how long would it take – ah – to – to kill him?

MANAGER: Nay, I canna tell ye. 'E didna seem to ha' strived much to get out – did he, Joe?

SECOND BEARER: No, not as far as Ah'n seen.

FIRST BEARER: You look at 'is 'ands, you'll see then. 'E'd non ha'e room to swing the pick.

 [*The* MANAGER *goes on his knees.*]

MRS HOLROYD [*shuddering*]: Oh, don't!

MANAGER: Ay, th' nails is broken a bit –

MRS HOLROYD [*clenching her fists*]: Don't!

MANAGER: 'E'd be sure ter ma'e a bit of a fight. But th' gas 'ud soon get hold on 'im. Ay, it's an awful thing to think of, it is indeed.

MRS HOLROYD [*her voice breaking*]: I can't bear it!

MANAGER: Eh, dear, we none on us know what's comin' next.

MRS HOLROYD [*getting hysterical*]: Oh, it's too awful, it's too awful!

BLACKMORE: You'll disturb the children.

GRANDMOTHER: And you don't want *them* down here.

MANAGER: 'E'd no business to ha' been left, you know.

RIGLEY: An' what man, dost think, wor goin' to sit him down on his hams an' wait for a chap as wouldna say 'thank yer' for his cump'ny? 'E'd bin ready to fall out wi' a flicker o' the candle, so who dost think wor goin' ter stop when we knowed 'e on'y kep on so's to get shut on us.

MANAGER: Tha'rt quite right, Bill, quite right. But theer you are.

RIGLEY: Ah' if we'd stopped, what good would it ha' done –

MANAGER: No, 'appen not, 'appen not.

RIGLEY: For, not known –

MANAGER: I'm sayin' nowt agen thee, neither one road nor t'other. [*There is general silence – then, to* MRS HOLROYD.] I should think th' inquest'll be at th' New Inn to-morrow, missis. I'll let you know.

MRS HOLROYD: Will there have to be an inquest?

MANAGER: Yes – there'll have to be an inquest. Shall you want anybody in, to stop with you to-night?

MRS HOLROYD: No.

MANAGER: Well, then, we'd best be goin'. I'll send my missis down first thing in the morning. It's a bad job, a bad job, it is. You'll be a' right then?

MRS HOLROYD: Yes.

MANAGER: Well, good night then – good night all.

ALL: Good night. Good night.

[*The* MANAGER, *followed by the two bearers, goes out, closing the door.*]

RIGLEY: It's like this, missis. I never should ha' gone, if he hadn't wanted us to.

MRS HOLROYD: Yes, I know.

RIGLEY: 'E wanted to come up by 's sen.

MRS HOLROYD [*wearily*]: I know how it was, Mr Rigley.

RIGLEY: Yes –

BLACKMORE: Nobody could foresee.

RIGLEY [*shaking his head*]: No. If there's owt, missis, as you want –

MRS HOLROYD: Yes – I think there isn't anything.

RIGLEY [*after a moment*]: Well – good night – we've worked i' the same stall ower four years now –

MRS HOLROYD: Yes.

RIGLEY: Well, good night, missis.

MRS HOLROYD AND BLACKMORE: Good night.

[*The* GRANDMOTHER *all this time has been rocking herself to and fro, moaning and murmuring beside the dead man. When* RIGLEY *has gone* MRS HOLROYD *stands staring distractedly before her. She has not yet looked at her husband.*]

GRANDMOTHER: Have you got the things ready, Lizzie?

MRS HOLROYD: What things?

GRANDMOTHER: To lay the child out.

MRS HOLROYD [*she shudders*]: No – what?

GRANDMOTHER: Haven't you put him by a pair o' white stockings, nor a white shirt?

MRS HOLROYD: He's got a white cricketing shirt – but not white stockings.

GRANDMOTHER: Then he'll have to have his father's. Let me look at the shirt, Lizzie. [MRS HOLROYD *takes one from the dresser drawer.*] This'll never do – a cold, canvas thing wi' a turndown collar. I s'll 'ave to fetch his father's. [*Suddenly.*] You don't want no other woman to touch him, to wash him and lay him out, do you?

MRS HOLROYD [*weeping*]: No.

GRANDMOTHER: Then I'll fetch him his father's gear. We mustn't let him set, he'll be that heavy, bless him. [*She takes her shawl.*] I shan't be more than a few minutes, an' the young fellow can stop here till I come back.

BLACKMORE: Can't I go for you, Mrs Holroyd?

GRANDMOTHER: No. *You* couldn't find the things. We'll wash him as soon as I get back, Lizzie.

MRS HOLROYD: Alright. [*She watches her mother-in-law go out. Then she starts, goes in the scullery for a bowl, in which she pours warm water. She takes a flannel and soap and towel. She stands, afraid to go any further.*]

BLACKMORE: Well!

MRS HOLROYD: This is a judgement on us.

BLACKMORE: Why?

MRS HOLROYD: On me, it is –

BLACKMORE: How?

MRS HOLROYD: It is.

[BLACKMORE *shakes his head.*]

MRS HOLROYD: Yesterday you talked of murdering him.

BLACKMORE: Well!

MRS HOLROYD: Now we've done it.

BLACKMORE: How?

MRS HOLROYD: He'd have come up with the others, if he hadn't felt – felt me murdering him.

BLACKMORE: But we can't help it.

MRS HOLROYD: It's my fault.

BLACKMORE: Don't be like that!

MRS HOLROYD [*looking at him – then indicating her husband*]: I daren't see him.

BLACKMORE: No?

MRS HOLROYD: I've killed him, that is all.

BLACKMORE: No, you haven't.

MRS HOLROYD: Yes, I have.

BLACKMORE: *We* couldn't help it.

MRS HOLROYD: If he hadn't felt, if he hadn't *known*, he wouldn't have stayed, he'd have come up with the rest.

BLACKMORE: Well, and even if it was so, we can't help it now.

MRS HOLROYD: But we've killed him.

BLACKMORE: Ah, I'm tired –

MRS HOLROYD: Yes.

BLACKMORE [*after a pause*]: Shall I stay?

MRS HOLROYD: I – I daren't be alone with him.

BLACKMORE [*sitting down*]: No.

MRS HOLROYD: I don't love him. Now he's dead. I don't love him. He lies like he did yesterday.

BLACKMORE: I suppose, being dead – I don't know –

MRS HOLROYD: I think you'd better go.

BLACKMORE [*rising*]: Tell me.

MRS HOLROYD: Yes.

BLACKMORE: You want me to go.

MRS HOLROYD: No – but *do* go. [*They look at each other.*]

BLACKMORE: I shall come to-morrow. [BLACKMORE *goes out.*]

[MRS HOLROYD *stands very stiff, as if afraid of the dead man. Then she stoops down and begins to sponge his face, talking to him.*]

MRS HOLROYD: My dear, my dear – oh, my dear! I can't bear it, my dear – you shouldn't have done it. You shouldn't have done it. Oh – I can't bear it, for you. Why couldn't I do anything for you? The children's father – my dear – I wasn't good to you. But you shouldn't have done this to me. Oh, dear, oh, dear! Did it hurt you? – oh, my dear, it hurt you – oh, I can't bear it. No, things aren't fair – we went wrong, my dear. I never loved you enough – I never did. What a shame for you! It was a shame. But you didn't – you didn't try. I *would* have loved you – I tried hard. What a shame for you! It was so cruel for you. You couldn't help it – my dear, my dear. You couldn't help it. And I can't do anything for you, and it hurt you so! [*She weeps bitterly, so her tears fall on the dead man's face; suddenly she kisses him.*] My dear, my dear, what can I do for you, what can I? [*She weeps as she wipes his face gently.*]

[*Enter* GRANDMOTHER.]

GRANDMOTHER [*putting a bundle on the table, and taking off her shawl*]: You're not all by yourself?

MRS HOLROYD: Yes.

GRANDMOTHER: It's a wonder you're not frightened. You've not washed his face.

MRS HOLROYD: Why should I be afraid of him – now, mother?

GRANDMOTHER [*weeping*]: Ay, poor lamb, I can't think as ever you could have had reason to be frightened of him, Lizzie.

MRS HOLROYD: Yes – once –

GRANDMOTHER: Oh, but he went wrong. An' he was a taking lad, as iver was. [*She cries pitifully.*] And when I waked his father up and told him, he sat up in bed staring over his whiskers, and said should he come up? But when I'd managed to find the shirt and things, he was still in bed. You don't know what it is to live with a man that has no feeling. But you've washed him, Lizzie?

198

MRS HOLROYD: I was finishing his head.

GRANDMOTHER: Let me do it, child.

MRS HOLROYD: I'll finish that.

GRANDMOTHER: Poor lamb – poor dear lamb! Yet I wouldn't wish him back, Lizzie. He must ha' died peaceful, Lizzie. He seems to be smiling. He always had such a rare smile on him – not that he's smiled much of late –

MRS HOLROYD: I loved him for that.

GRANDMOTHER: Ay, my poor child – my poor child.

MRS HOLROYD: He looks nice, mother.

GRANDMOTHER: I hope he made his peace with the Lord.

MRS HOLROYD: Yes.

GRANDMOTHER: If he hadn't time to make his peace with the Lord, I've no hopes of him. Dear o' me, dear o' me. Is there another bit of flannel anywhere?

[MRS HOLROYD *rises and brings a piece. The* GRAND-MOTHER *begins to wash the breast of the dead man.*]

GRANDMOTHER: Well, I hope you'll be true to his children at least, Lizzie.

[MRS HOLROYD *weeps – the old woman continues her washing.*]
Eh – and he's fair as a lily. Did you ever see a man with a whiter skin – and flesh as fine as the driven snow. He's beautiful, he is, the lamb. Many's the time I've looked at him, and I've felt proud of him, I have. And now·he lies here. And such arms on 'im! Look at the vaccination marks, Lizzie. When I took him to be vaccinated, he had a little pink bonnet with a feather. [*Weeps.*] Don't cry, my girl, don't. Sit up an' wash him a' that side, or we s'll never have him done. Oh, Lizzie!

MRS HOLROYD [*sitting up, startled*]: What – what?

GRANDMOTHER: Look at his poor hand! [*She holds up the right hand. The nails are bloody.*]

MRS HOLROYD: Oh, no! Oh, no! No!

[*Both women weep.*]

GRANDMOTHER [*after a while*]: We maun get on, Lizzie.

MRS HOLROYD [*sitting up*]: I can't touch his hands.

GRANDMOTHER: But I'm his mother – there's nothing I couldn't do for him.

MRS HOLROYD: I don't care – I don't care.

GRANDMOTHER: Prithee, prithee, Lizzie, I don't want thee goin' off, Lizzie.

MRS HOLROYD [*moaning*]: Oh, what shall I do!

GRANDMOTHER: Why, go thee an' get his feet washed. He's setting stiff, and how shall we get him laid out?

[MRS HOLROYD, *sobbing, goes, kneels at the miner's feet, and begins pulling off the great boots.*]

GRANDMOTHER: There's hardly a mark on him. Eh, what a man he is! I've had some fine sons, Lizzie, I've had some big men of sons.

MRS HOLROYD: He was always a lot whiter than me. And he used to chaff me.

GRANDMOTHER: But his poor hands! I used to thank God for my children, but they're rods o' trouble, Lizzie, they are. Unfasten his belt, child. We mun get his things off soon, or else we s'll have such a job.

[MRS HOLROYD, *having dragged off the boots, rises. She is weeping.*]

CURTAIN